WITHDRAWN

Writing Against Time

Books by Howard Moss

CRITICISM
Writing Against Time   1969
The Magic Lantern of Marcel Proust   1962

POEMS
Second Nature   1968
Finding Them Lost   1965
A Winter Come, A Summer Gone   1960
A Swimmer in the Air   1957
The Toy Fair   1954
The Wound and the Weather   1946

EDITED, WITH AN INTRODUCTION
The Nonsense Books of Edward Lear   1963
Keats   1959

WRITING AGAINST TIME

Critical Essays and Reviews by

HOWARD MOSS

PS
3525
.08638
W7

William Morrow and Company, Inc.

New York 1969

 X80096

ST. PAUL PUBLIC LIBRARY

Copyright © 1969 by Howard Moss

Dylan Thomas: A Broadcast, from *A Casebook on Dylan Thomas,* reprinted by permission of Thomas Y. Crowell Company and WBAI.

John Keats: An Introduction, from *The Laurel Keats,* reprinted by permission of Dell Publishing Co., Inc. Copyright © 1959 by Richard Wilbur.

Daniel Fuchs: Homage to the Thirties, reprinted by permission of The New Yorker Magazine, Inc. Copyright 1961 by Howard Moss.

Katherine Anne Porter: No Safe Harbor, reprinted by permission of The New Yorker Magazine, Inc. Copyright 1962 by Howard Moss.

John Keats: The Noose of the Whole, reprinted by permission of The New York Times Company. Copyright © 1963 by The New York Times Company. First published under the title "His Own Greatness He Did Not Recognize" in *The New York Times Book Review.*

Anton Chekhov: The Desert Everywhere, reprinted by permission of The New Yorker Magazine, Inc. Copyright 1963 by Howard Moss.

Nathalie Sarraute: Make It Vague, reprinted by permission of *The Kenyon Review.* Copyright © 1963 by Kenyon College.

Edward Lear: An Introduction, from *The Nonsense Book of Edward Lear,* reprinted by permission of New American Library, Inc. Copyright 1964 by The New American Library, Inc.

Denis Devlin: Christ in the Machine, from *The Selected Devlin,* reprinted by permission of *The Sewanee Review.* Copyright 1964 by The University of the South.

Katherine Anne Porter: Reversing the Binoculars, reprinted by permission of The New York Times Company. Copyright © 1965 by The New York Times Company. First published under the title "A Poet of The Story" in *The New York Times Book Review.*

Elizabeth Bishop: All Praise, reprinted by permission of *The Kenyon Review.* Copyright © 1966 by Kenyon College.

Henry James: The Imperial Theme, from "Notes on Fiction," Wisconsin Studies in Contemporary Literature, reprinted by permission of the copyright owners, the Regents of the University of Wisconsin.

Proust, Chekhov, James, Mann, from "Notes on Fiction," Wisconsin Studies in Contemporary Literature, reprinted by permission of the copyright owners, the Regents of the University of Wisconsin.

Glenway Wescott: Love Birds of Prey, reprinted by permission of The New Yorker Magazine, Inc. Copyright 1967 by Howard Moss.

Dylan Thomas: A Thin, Curly Little Person, reprinted by permission of The New Yorker Magazine, Inc. Copyright 1967 by Howard Moss.

Lois Moyles: An Introduction, reprinted by permission of WORKS.

A Contribution to a Symposium, reprinted by permission of *South Dakota Review,* copyright 1967 by South Dakota Review.

Flann O'Brien: Tom Swift in Hell, reprinted by permission of The New Yorker Magazine, Inc. Copyright 1968 by Howard Moss.

Elizabeth Bowen: Intelligence at War, reprinted by permission of The New York Times Company. Copyright © 1968 by The New York Times Company. First published under the title "The Heiress Is an Outsider" in *The New York Times Book Review.*

All rights reserved. No part of this book may be reproduced or utilized in any form or by any means, electronic or mechanical, including photocopying, recording or by any information storage and retrieval system, without permission in writing from the Publisher. Inquiries should be addressed to William Morrow and Company, Inc., 105 Madison Ave., New York, N.Y. 10016

Printed in the United States of America

Library of Congress Catalog Card Number 74-80910

For Maeve Brennan

Introductory Note

THE DIFFERING LENGTHS of these pieces—*The Golden Bowl,* a long novel, gets less space than *The Pilgrim Hawk,* a short one—are not meant to suggest any kind of evaluation.

The pages on *The Golden Bowl* originally formed part of *Proust, Chekhov, James, Mann: Notes on Fiction.* Reading them over, they seemed too long to qualify as a note and not long enough to shape up as an essay. Not wanting to lose them, I simply excerpted them and let them stand on their own.

The chapters on Tolstoy and Shakespeare have not been published before.

The Theater, The New, and The Now: A Letter was actually written as a letter but was never sent and never published. After reading an article in a literary quarterly written by a fellow member of the Playwrights' Unit, I wrote a reply. And though I mentioned it to the quarterly's editor, she informed me that there would be little point in sending it since the next issue was devoted to French writers, and by the time the issue after *that* appeared (the magazine is published sporadically), the relevance of my letter might be obscure to the readers. Since it says some things I believe, I have included it here. Because it was never published, it seemed unfair to me to use the name of the writer of the original article. I refer to him as Mr. L.

These essays and reviews are arranged chronologically in the order of their composition.

Contents

Writing Against Time

Dylan Thomas
A Broadcast

The word *human* is the one most commonly used when people try to define the qualities of Dylan Thomas's personality. And it is a sad commentary on what the rest of us are that the word should be used as a mark of distinction. Hackneyed as it is as a description, it is not without its truth. For Dylan Thomas was human in a way most people are not. The adulation and derogation he suffered were the symptoms of his being himself. Sober or drunk, he was more awake than most people ever are or become.

His importance to the many people he knew during his lifetime was a token of both a real and a spurious distinction: Thomas by being himself appeared to his audience to be a rebel. And it is a notorious fact that rebellion, unaccompanied by either talent or genius, is dangerous and sometimes fatal. Thomas's genius made him a safe symbol for other people's instincts for rebellion. To put it simply, everyone was secretly glad that *some*one was being himself and getting away with it.

Being oneself exacts a price most people cannot afford to pay. Thomas paid it. To say that he did not take his life into his own hands would be untrue. He seemed to want to be what he was; whether that was a free choice or not, no one can say. But to see him as a martyr, as many people do, is to distort the truth. Thomas enjoyed, or seemed to, his role; he left himself open to the kind of "story" he was to become; and if he was used by others in the pursuit of such gain, it is only fair to say that he used others, too.

Thomas left no one untouched who met him. For there was another side to him that accounts, in part, for the enormous pull of his personality. If he was a rebel, he was also a child. And his friends paid for their symbol by having to take care of it. The great howl that arose upon his death might be genuinely explained by the fact that a fine poet had died at the age of thirty-nine. Surely that is a matter for grief. But there was another reason for the general uproar: no one wanted to believe that there is a price to pay for romantic indulgence, or put another way, a profligate sickness, and it was hard for many of his followers to understand that a lifetime of drinking can result in death from alcohol. Thomas, who had a fondness for Third Avenue bars, could believe it. He was not a romantic symbol to himself.

That he saw himself as he was only made him the more illusory to people who insisted on his being an illusion. That Thomas's misbehavior, so-called, was more than a wanton flouting of convention is obvious. It was the nature of his "misbehavior" that made him irresistible to so many people.

He was not afraid to ask for what he wanted. When he was bored with literature and wanted life, he asked for that, too. And it was from the exercise of simple rights that Thomas started to become a legend. For who among us dares to ask for what he wants, dares to say what he means, dares to live a life that is interesting to him rather than to a thousand other people?

None of this alone would explain Thomas's aura. He was singular in his gifts for life as well as poetry. He was a spellbinding storyteller, an inexhaustible fountain of verbal invention, and a marvelous mimic and actor. He had no respect for sham and pretension, even when they were masked as humility, and he was rarely boring. Being genuinely kind and loving, he seemed unique to those people who believe that kindness and love are moral qualities.

I think it would also be true to say that it was partly his adolescence that made him attractive to adolescents. That he was a highly civilized and sophisticated one merely confused the unwary who cannot believe that so many attributes can be combined in one person. To hide the fact that Thomas was often a chore and a burden to those who loved him the most would be a lie. And it should be obvious that they did not love him because he was a chore and a burden. He was, as most of us are not, a person. He was funny, enchanting, and alive.

That he hurt people is axiomatic. Whether it was worth it to them is their business. That they hurt him is axiomatic, too. It has been a long time since such a phenomenon made an appearance. But the phenomenon seems more special in that we are, most of us, so pedestrian. And it is—and will increasingly become so—only of interest to those who actually knew him as a person whether he was a victim of himself, or of the world that victimizes everyone. The truth is that he was a poet who left us magnificent poems. For that, we should be grateful.

[1958]

John Keats
An Introduction

When a poet becomes a legend, his poems are obscured; the man becomes more important than his work. Keats was particularly unfortunate in this respect. The metamorphosis of Keats, poet into hero, is not difficult to understand. He was what once would have been called, without embarrassment, a great spirit, and his life fulfills the most extravagant notions of genius tried by adversity. Events scarred a personality vulnerable to their harshness, articulate as to their meaning, and strong enough not to be vanquished. Disaster dogged him: the early death of his parents; the responsibility for his younger brothers— one hopelessly ill, the other emigrated to America and in financial difficulties—the separation from his sister enforced by her guardian; a vicious attack on his work; a miserably unhappy love affair; and the final horrors of disease, isolation, and premature death. By the time Keats died of tuberculosis in Rome at the age of twenty-six, these well-known facts were already being picked over, and they have been examined, annotated, and rehashed ever since. Keats's life is a convenient prototype. The legend truly feeds on fact. But legend needs more than fact; it requires ambiguity. This is supplied, in Keats's case, by a special circumstance: the existence and quality of his letters. For the Keats of the poems and the Keats of the letters are not the same. In the effort to reconcile them, critics have made up many versions of Keats. Because mystery and documentation exist side by side to an unparalleled degree, Keats presents one of the most tempting puzzles of scholarship and criticism.

Considering the documentation we have, why should Keats remain elusive? There are four reasons.

1: *Keats is the poet of youth.* If we read Keats when young, as we generally do, we are met by an accommodating condition: most of what Keats had to say that challenged the intellect is said in the letters, not in the poems. The poems have an immediacy that readily promotes, in the adolescent mind, notions of what the "poetic" should be: musical, atmospheric, melancholy, moody. We do not have to dig far beneath the surface to be enchanted by them. There is something magical in the sound of Keats's language, in the remoteness of many of his pictorial effects, that naïve perception can fasten on instantly. And because we sense Keats before we know him, we are inclined to remember him vaguely. We do not, in the earliest stage of our lives as readers, want to know or to be told what Keats "means." This approach to poetry has its limitations: It overemphasizes sentimentality and superficial effects, and unless it is absorbed and outgrown, poetry remains a matter of credulous magic. This early *remembered* feeling about Keats tends to obscure what is actually down on paper.

2: *The uneven quality of the poems.* Keats's development covered a short span of time and his maturation as an artist was erratic. The period of the great poems, the Odes, "The Eve of St. Agnes," "Lamia"—the period between January and May, 1819—hangs in space, a kind of miracle between his immature work and the inferior work that followed it, with the exception of the first half of the revision of *Hyperion* and "To Autumn." I think Keats's reputation would be as secure as it is today if we had no other poems than these. But these great moments in Keats are repeated only in *parts* of the other poems; the variation in quality exists not only between one poem and another but often within one poem itself. These ups and downs in Keats force us to break up the poems into lines, phrases, and stanzas. We have a few magnificent poems and then patches of a similar magnificence throughout. The total effect is one of diffusion. (We do not have this effect in Donne, Milton, or Blake.)

3: *Keats's temperament.* Keats, in describing the poetical character in a letter to Richard Woodhouse (October 27, 1818), describes himself:

As to the Poetical Character itself (I mean that sort of which, if I am anything, I am a Member . . .) it is not itself—it has no self—it is every thing and nothing— It has no character—it enjoys light and shade; it lives in gusto, be it foul or fair, high or low, rich or poor, mean or elevated . . . A Poet is the most unpoetical thing in existence; because

he has no Identity . . . not one word I ever utter
can be taken for granted as an opinion growing
out of my identical nature—how can it, since I
have no nature?

If we believe this statement, we cannot, of course,
take it literally. The statement warns us against doing
so, for here is an opinion that asks us to distrust it. And
there is something else wrong with it, too, we feel.
Keats comes to us as a vivid and distinct personality,
not as a person without "identity" or "nature." But it
is both revealing and symptomatic that Keats should
have thought this, and it provides us with an important clue to what we can and cannot understand about
him. He is vivid, but it is a vividness of fused contrasts.
The "light" and "shade" in Keats are not easily distinguished. In describing a passage from *Paradise Lost,*
Keats uses the phrases "black brightness" and "ebon
diamonding." What he says of Milton we may say of
him. Experience is seen as a welding of opposites:
shade and light, energy and indolence, lucidity and
vagueness. It does not surprise us to come upon lines
like "Welcome joy and welcome sorrow," or "Ay, in
the very temple of Delight / Veil'd Melancholy has her
sovran shrine," or "Do I wake or sleep?" This *feeling*
in Keats of two states of mind ordinarily in opposition
being sensed at the same time, taken together with the
explicit interest in ideas expressed in the letters, leads
us to expect some final resolution, some grand summing up of thought that never materializes. An extraordinarily perceptive mind, one sensitive to motive,
implication, and correspondences, is not the same as a

conceptual intelligence. The temptation to derive universal truths from statements of Keats that apply specifically to himself has muddied the fact that many of the things he said were applicable only to himself and were parts of a process of thinking rather than ultimate conclusions. This "translation" of specific feelings into general thoughts has made it more difficult to understand what Keats really thought and felt.

4: *Keats's use of abstractions and generalizations.* Here are three statements by Keats, the first two from letters, the last from "Ode on a Grecian Urn." a: "The Imagination may be compared to Adam's dream—he awoke and found it truth." b: "O for a life of Sensations rather than of Thoughts!" c: " 'Beauty is truth, truth beauty.' "

These statements are taken out of context. But even in context, we are forced to flounder over the definition of these words; we cannot say, ultimately, what Keats meant by them. The real difficulty is this: Though each of these notions may be seen as part of an argument against abstraction, the argument is vitiated by being itself advanced in abstractions. It is through his *feelings,* and not his *theory* of feelings that we understand whatever we do about Keats. He is a major poet; he is a remarkable human being; he is not a psychologist or a philosopher.

It is necessary to make a distinction, particularly in the letters, between two kinds of thought in Keats: insights and concepts—the former brilliant intuitions and illuminations of the human condition, the latter attempts to systematize ideas into an abstract and all-embracing theory. An example of an insight:

Our imaginary woes are conjured up by our passions, and are fostered by passionate feeling; our
real ones come of themselves, and are opposed by
an abstract exertion of mind. Real grievances are
displacers of passion. The imaginary nail a man
down for a sufferer, as on the cross; the real spur
him up into an agent. . . .

   (*Letter to Charles Brown, September 23, 1819.*)

An example of a concept:

This point I sincerely wish to consider because I
think it a grander system of salvation than the
chrystain [Christian] religion—or rather it is a
system of Spirit-creation— This is effected by three
grand materials acting the one upon the other for
a series of years. These three Materials are the
Intelligence—the *human heart* (as distinguished
from intelligence or Mind) and the *World* or *El-
emental space* suited for the purpose of forming
the *Soul* or *Intelligence destined to possess the
sense of Identity**. . . .

   (*Letter to George and Georgiana Keats, Febru-
   ary 14 to May 3, 1819.*)

---

* The following passage succeeds immediately the one quoted.
In order to make his meaning clear, it seems, Keats switches
from the use of conceptual words to metaphor. " . . . I can
scarcely express what I but dimly perceive—and yet I think
I perceive it. That you may judge the more clearly, I will put
it in the most homely form possible. I will call the *world* a
school instituted for the purpose of teaching little children to
read. I will call the *human heart* the *horn book* used in that

Keats has been at the mercy of two contrasting views. In one, best summed up by Yeats's notion of him as a boy with his face pressed against the window of a sweetshop, he is an adolescent, all sensation and appetite. In the other, of which C. D. Thorpe is the most cogent spokesman, Keats is a Platonic idealist, who believes that through a mounting succession of sensations we arrive at those essences that make up reality. Neither of these views is without point; neither is adequate to the case.

Yeats suggests a key word, particularly in regard to the early Keats: *sweet.* The senses, primarily oral, secondarily tactile, gorging on the luxuries of the world, dominate the imagery. The "slippery blisses," "moist kisses," and "creamy breasts" have not escaped notice. The abundance of nymphs and satyrs got up in lush nature costumes, the debased Greek decoration, softness of tone, muddiness of diction, lapses of taste— all these have been the subject of censure. But no mere boy with a sweet tooth could have written the Odes or the great letters. Yeats hits on Keats's major weakness, excess, but the view he stands for here tells us the worst about Keats and ignores the best.

Mr. Thorpe is by no means unconvincing. There is

---

school, and I will call the *child able to read,* the *soul* made from that *school* and its *horn book.* Do you see how necessary a world of pains and troubles is to school an intelligence and make it a soul? A place where the heart must feel and suffer in a thousand diverse ways! Not merely is the heart a horn book, it is the mind's bible, it is the mind's experience, it is the teat from which the mind or intelligence sucks its identity. . . ."

a good deal of evidence to support the idea that Keats was a Platonic idealist of sorts. But only of sorts. There is one major drawback to this theory: Keats did not move in any continuous process from appetites to essences. Unlike Plato's or Dante's vision of love, Keats's was split at the beginning and split at the end. Keats's vision was double, not a steady clarification. Mr. Thorpe's argument is more a corrective to Yeats's viewpoint than really valid on its own. Keats does not seem to be, from the evidence, either a high priest of the senses or a profound philosopher. He is sensuous, even sensual—most poets are—and he died young. He thinks; he thinks brilliantly; but to strain some coherent world view out of the letters and the poems is to force their meaning. It would be safe to say that, in his early life at least, he wanted to believe there was an implicit process in nature that led, by steps, to some moral conclusion; sensation led to love, and experience to knowledge. And one might say, roughly, that the subject of *Endymion* is love, and of *Hyperion* knowledge. But *Endymion* was a conceded failure, and *Hyperion* was never finished. It seems likely that Keats could not finish *Hyperion* because he was increasingly uncertain of this natural, moral progression in nature and experience. To argue that Keats was either a sensualist or an idealist is to miss the point that his temperament was the battleground on which sensations and ideas clashed but were never reconciled. The resulting double vision was, at first, the *method* by which Keats perceived his material. Finally, it became the *subject* of his maturest work.

Keats struggled with forms that were inimical to him: the epic, the play, the narrative poem. He lacked three prerequisites for narration and drama: a: the ability to depersonalize himself (though he recognized its value); b: control over character and plotting; c: the sense of a great design that is necessary in epic poetry and heroic drama. It is the mark of the failure of *Endymion,* for instance, that we can fish its major theme out of a small portion of the sea. Just before the poem ends, the moon goddess ("ideal beauty") conveniently merges with the Indian Lady ("real" or "sensuous beauty"). After four thousand lines, we discover that the "supersensuous" and the "sensuous" are, and always were, really one. We do not believe it, just as we remain unconvinced by the characters, who do not have, in any dramatic sense, psychologies or consciences, or, in any epic sense, importance. Thought, in *Endymion,* is extraneous; we have no sense of its having grown organically out of the action.

In *Hyperion,* the difficulty is conceptual. There is often a ring of Miltonic sureness to the blank verse, and occasionally merely an echo of it. But after Keats has described the plight of the old Titans, he switches to a new god, Apollo, and breaks off. He is either uncertain of his subject or becoming aware of its falsity *for him*. He does not seem to know quite what to do with his new Olympians. Are they to be grander, sadder, wiser than the Titans they have overthrown? A tragic situation is depicted, not dramatized, and, though we have reached Book III, we find ourselves still in the exposition of a complicated plot whose outlines remain conjectural.

In "The Eve of St. Agnes," Keats has solved at least one difficulty by narrowing his range from the epic to the narrative poem. "The Eve of St. Agnes" is a masterpiece of artificial atmosphere. But even in it, the most famous and highly praised of his narrative poems, he is not yet the mature Keats. Some of its best scenes are irrelevant to the action—the scene, for instance, in which Porphyro sets the table before Madeline awakes. It is a brilliant scene and provides an extraordinary contrast to the snow, cold, and darkness outside. But it is a *painted* scene, not an *acted* one. "The Eve of St. Agnes" is remarkable for its word-painting rather than for anything else. Its triumph is one of language, but language only—a great triumph, yet not the one that Keats was ultimately to have.

By the time we get to "Lamia," a great deal has happened to Keats. He has read Dryden, for one, and the couplets are controlled and varied. He has had some sense of failure at the epic, some sense of success at the narrative poem. But, up to this point, the epics deal with myth, the narrative poems with legend. In "Lamia," he successfully combines myth and narration. "Lamia" is symbolically weighted; it is not a tale told merely for the sake of the telling. The action hinges on a simple recognition scene; the theme is strikingly similar to that of *Endymion*, but has taken on new dimensions and is more convincingly resolved. The conclusion is pessimistic; that is, the ending is not false. Apollonius, the philosopher, reveals to Lycius, the hero, that his betrothed, Lamia, is, in reality, a serpent. Lamia vanishes; Lycius dies. The division between the "intellect" and the "senses" is clearly dramatized.

(In "Isabella," written a year and a half earlier than "Lamia," it hardly seems accidental that Keats should have chosen to set into verse a Boccaccio story in which the heroine keeps her murdered lover's *head* in a pot of basil, where she carefully nurtures it. The head and body of Lorenzo, the hero of "Isabella," are literally severed.) The "real" Lamia and the "ideal" Lamia are not allowed to merge. Apollonius sees the magic lurking behind Lamia's beauty, but the point of the poem is ambiguous. Apollonius is described both as a "philosopher" and a "sophist," and there is a specific attack on philosophy as the killer of beauty. ("Do not all charms fly / At the mere touch of cold philosophy?") Nevertheless, though Apollonius destroys the relationship and kills "gentle" Lamia, she is presented to us as a woman, a goddess, and a serpent. The poem seems to suggest in its action that though the bemused lover sees the goddess in the woman, the rational intellect will always detect the serpent in the goddess. Magic, which has been benevolent in the other poems, here shows traces of evil. Apollonius may be the villain, but it is hard to escape the conclusion that he reveals the truth, and that, where love is concerned, the truth is destructive. The intellect may see through and destroy magic. What we are not sure of is whether magic is good or evil in itself. Despite this uncertainty, "Lamia" is the best of Keats's long poems. It is the only one which exhibits technical mastery throughout and in which the action is at the service of the theme. It belongs, in accomplishment, with the Odes and "The Eve of St. Agnes."

The idea that sensual beauty is overwhelming but

incompatible with ideal beauty, that physical love cannot attain to the poet's conception of ideal love is central to Keats. But there is a larger preoccupation behind this theme: the connection Keats makes between art and life and death and love. This essential notion, developing throughout Keats's work, sometimes as an attitude, sometimes as a subject, reaches its final sounding in the two great Odes, "To a Nightingale," and "On a Grecian Urn." The urn ode is Keats's final statement on his vision of the Greek experience. If the poem defines the supremacy of art over life, there is a melancholy undertone that affects its meaning. It is a nostalgic poem. The artist's experience of ecstasy may be preserved in a work of art, but at a great sacrifice: the direct experience of life itself. To go beyond the senses may be to capture them forever—but in their captivity, the senses are apprehended differently. The freedom art affords is also a prison. There is a profound irony underlying the subject: the figures on the urn not only outlast what they depict, they transform it. For life to be made permanent, it must be sacrificed. And it is perhaps significant that, of the two scenes on the urn, one should be a sacrifice itself. (There are two separate scenes on the urn, not a continuous one such as that described on the Grecian urn in the "Ode on Indolence." C. M. Bowra, in *The Romantic Imagination,* says, intriguingly, that Keats, in using these two separated scenes, may have anticipated Nietzsche's division of Greek culture into the Apollonian and Dionysian modes.) Keats exhorts the lover in stanza two in two ways: "Bold Lover, never, never canst thou kiss . . ." And later, "She cannot fade, though thou hast not thy bliss, / For ever wilt thou love, and she be fair!" If time is arrested, physical passion must remain frustrated. If physical passion is fulfilled, time will ultimately destroy it. It is the artist who transmutes these irreconcilables. And the "Ode on a Grecian Urn" is more correctly read as a poem on the experience of the artist that goes into the making of a work of art than as a poem on the work of art itself.

In the "Ode to a Nightingale," Keats's masterpiece, there is a crucial shift. Keats becomes "I"—not the adolescent "I" of "I stood tip-toe upon a little hill," or the human "I" of the letters, marvelous as that may be. It is the "I" of the mature poet in relation to his great theme, his own consciousness.

There are two arguments in the ode. 1: The real versus the ideal nature of the nightingale's song; 2: The real or ideal nature of the nightingale's song versus an actual world of pain, suffering, and death.

Argument 1: The nightingale's song emerges from the physical body of a real bird. The *song* is immortal; the individual nightingale that produces it is not. Because the song is the ostensible subject of the poem, the bird need not be visible. It is possible, at any moment, for the bird to fly away—for the song to cease. We have, then, an appropriate symbol for Keats's real-ideal dichotomy: a physical entity that creates beauty, is equally of the earth and of the sky, is unseen but heard, and is historically connected with the idea of *ideal* beauty.

There is a further and profound complication. The symbol is mirrored in the perceiver. The "I" of the

poem is literally *entranced*. We do not know whether
he is awake or asleep, whether the poem is dream or
vision. Two questions interlock: Can a bird produce a
song so beautiful that it transcends the bird's physical
existence in time? Does a listener, hearing the song,
still exist in that same reality of which he was a part
before he heard the song—a reality he knows, from
another level of experience, to be mundane, sequential,
and physical? Before these two questions may be
asked, it is necessary to modify the reader's ordinary
conception of time. In order for the symbolic transac-
tion between the nightingale and the listener to occur,
they must both be rooted in physical reality and freed
from it. The trance the narrator is in at the beginning of
the poem, and to which he returns at the end, allows
Keats to release his protagonist from time. The real and
the ideal are as operative in the perceiver as in what he
perceives. The nightingale is the object of the poem;
consciousness is its subject.

Argument 2: Consciousness is not able to escape its
limitations, but in recognizing the fact, it is able to
transcend them. The ordinary, mortal world of stanza
three, "where men sit and hear each other groan; /
Where palsy shakes a few, sad, last gray hairs, / Where
youth grows pale, and spectre-thin, and dies," is the
world, finally, in which the perceiver must live and
die. *But it is also the world in which he hears the nightingale's song.* If the narrator were really able to fly
away with the nightingale, to escape from his reality,
either "charioted by Bacchus and his pards," or "on
the viewless wings of Poesy," he would do so at the
expense of the very experience he is undergoing. For

there is no ideal perceiver—even in a state of trance, he remains aware of the world of stanza three. And without the world of stanza three, the nightingale's song might be neither beautiful nor ideal. The two arguments merge: immortality is rooted in mortality; the nightingale's timeless song is heard by a man who must exist in time. The narrator is made aware of the timelessness of the nightingale's song by the very fact of his existence in time.

[1959]

Daniel Fuchs
Homage
to the Thirties

H umiliation, as the theme of a minority-group novel, is one of the hardest subjects in the world for a writer to see in perspective. He must have felt it to want to write about it; he must be free of it to be able to. If it still rankles, the writer is in no position to see clearly. If it is glossed over, he forfeits his material. He can resort to two stereotyped evasions: the novel of special pleading, in which the characters, by virtue of belonging to the group, are made more lovable than we know them to be, and the novel of social significance, in which they start out as typical, turn into heroes, and end up incredible. To see humiliation from a comic viewpoint is rare. It is less a matter of self-knowledge and dispassion than of temperament. The slum life of Brooklyn Jews, a life of poverty and debasement, is anything but intrinsically funny, and from a social point of view it is tragic. It is the par-

ticular triumph of Daniel Fuchs that in three novels
written on the subject in the thirties, and now reissued
—*Summer in Williamsburg, Homage to Blenholt,* and
Low Company—his characters are neither too charming nor too heroic. Moreover, they are often marvelously funny.

Summer in Williamsburg, the earliest of the novels,
is the least comic, the most personal, and the least
certain. It is a novel about a tenement and what goes
on inside it. One suicide begins it, another ends it;
between these parentheses, the action is a simple conflict. Label Hayman—the first of Fuchs's gentle, put-
upon fathers—is good, honest, and a failure. Uncle
Papravel, a racketeer, is dishonest and a success. Hayman's two sons, Philip and Harry, are torn between
these opposed views of life, one moral and stagnant,
the other workable and self-damaging. It is a problem
dear to the first-generation novel, whether it is Jewish,
Irish, or Italian. Money is an overpowering hypnotic
for Fuchs's characters: for Mrs. Linck, the janitress,
whose apartment is filled with guinea pigs that slide
around in the dark; for Old Miller, the miser, who
hides his bankbooks under floorboards and is finally
swindled in a diamond deal; for Tessie, Philip's unsteady girlfriend, who lives her life as if it were a movie
but marries a ladies'-underwear salesman. Money here
is more than the solution to poverty; it is the overcom-
ing of a deeply felt hurt. It is one thing to be hungry,
another to be hungry and unloved, and something else
again to be hungry and despised. Fuchs's slum dwellers
want, like most people, to be rich (or safe) and loved.
More important, they want to be *recognized*. Recogni-

tion requires visibility. Money not only talks but can be made to be seen. But if love is a psychological solvent, and money a social one, neither is a guarantee of recognition—if by recognition you mean that unquestioning look of approval the world sometimes gives back. The young, confused intellectuals of Fuchs's first two novels feel this keenly without being able to put their finger on the source of their uneasiness. They are offered honesty-and-poverty or dishonesty-and-wealth. What they really long for is to overcome the world's indifference. After a scarring adolescent love affair, Philip is left dangling, unable to make a choice. Harry, who has been one of Uncle Papravel's gangster henchmen, quits and becomes a tie salesman. Fuchs is honest in not offering us a solution, but—in one respect, at least—he is still unsatisfactory as a novelist. Even an insoluble problem can be made dramatic, and Fuchs, in his first novel, does not yet know how to tell a story.

Summer in Williamsburg is a rhapsodic book; it contains the largest quantity of felt life of all three novels. But it is more random collage than construction. It is filled with the sights, sounds, and smells of the streets, the pungency of Jewish idiom, and an absolutely sure sense of the physical look and social meaning of institutions—the candy store, the street gang, the social club. Though Fuchs knows that the daydream is the most powerful force behind action, he still doesn't know what to do with it. He is, in this book, an observer longing for a point of view. His most enchanting character is Cohen, a useless, mocked writer of intellectual pretensions. (Cohen's play is first called *The Whoremonger,* then *The Harlot-Master,* and finally

Green Gods in Yellow.) It is the character of Cohen who shows Fuchs the way out. In one scene, Cohen is dressed in a rented tuxedo on the way to a party. He loses the girl he is escorting in a subway crush. At the party, he is sent off to retrieve a jar of herring someone forgot to bring. Cohen gets it, takes a taxi back (a very unusual experience for him), and, in his excitement, drops the herring, which spills over his rented suit. In despair, he tries to commit suicide by jumping off a bridge, but is fished out of the water by a man on a passing barge. The special combination of the real and the absurd, a form of slapstick that is to become Fuchs's trademark, is here in embryo.

In all of Fuchs's novels, someone is going to the movies, trying to go to the movies, at the movies, or thinking of going. The antidote to the nightmare is the daydream. The terror of economic squalor is helplessness, and the heroines and heroes of the movies are free to make choices that Philip and Tessie, for instance, are not. Fuchs, who must have gone to the movies as often as his characters, learned from them something his characters never needed to know: the unconscious power of the movies lies not only in their content but in the medium itself. No matter what image they present, they attack reality in a basic way by dissolving its strongest cement, the everyday relationship of cause and effect. They manipulate time as if it were not consecutive and space as if the impossibly near and the impossibly far were within visual range. Fuchs, naturally compassionate, naturally ironic, was looking for a way of handling his material. According to his preface—splendid in its modesty, relevance, and brevity—he was aware as early as *Summer in Williamsburg* of the necessity of form; at the same time, he wanted to be true to life. The two things seemed either incompatible or beyond his powers, but for an inherently comic writer who was also a moviegoer, slapstick was ready to hand. Muteness and violence are two of its ingredients; they are all the funnier for ordinarily not being funny at all, and they connect seriously with life. Muteness, an early technical drawback of the movie camera, automatically excluded verbal wit. Silence has little value for a novelist. Fuchs sought out its equivalent: his characters do not know how to say what they mean; often they do not even *know* what they mean. In dialogue, the tensions exerted by these two human failings can become a form of significant muteness. (In the theater of the forties and fifties, the device was extended until it became absurd; playwrights got stuck with the inarticulate hero. He had something to say but he couldn't talk. The result was several celebrated plays that were, in reality, long intermissions.) As for violence, the camera has two advantages that can enhance or dissipate its impact: in space, the closeup; in time, the ability to speed up or slow down action. The enhancement of violence is pointless in comedy. In slapstick, violence is always harmless; its comic-strip characters are hit over the head but never land in the hospital with a concussion. Fuchs's scenes of violence—the destruction of a bus station in *Summer in Williamsburg,* Moe Karty being beaten up by his brothers-in-law in *Low Company*—are oddly similar. He describes violence with great accuracy; nevertheless, there is always a

certain distance and disinterestedness. We watch each
scene as if we were looking at a good dogfight—concerned, but aware of its absurdity. Aside from finding
slapstick the solution to technical difficulties, Fuchs
understood its message very well: the world doesn't
work for one's benefit. It was the same conclusion he
had arrived at in *Summer in Williamsburg,* in which
the matter and the form fell apart. In *Homage to Blenholt,* the subject and the method say the same thing.

The Philip Hayman of the earlier book becomes
Max Balkan in *Homage to Blenholt*—another young
dreamer, this time one who thinks up get-rich-quick
schemes and sends them off in the mail to large com-
panies. Cohen, a character in the first book unconnected with its narrative conflict, is moved to stage
center and transformed into Mendel Munves, an amateur etymologist, who knows "not only all possible
languages but also all the dialects of each." And the
sinister but attractive gangsters and gamblers randomly
strung throughout *Summer in Williamsburg* are rolled
into Coblenz, a hard-drinking horseplayer tortured by
a toothache and a passel of kids who roller-skate in
the apartment above him. For the two suicides that
form a thematic thread in *Williamsburg* we have, more
appropriately, the attempts of Max's girlfriend, Ruth,
to persuade him to see a Joan Crawford movie at the
Miramar. Max doesn't want to go to the movies. A
funeral is to be held for Blenholt, the former commissioner of sewers, and Max admires Blenholt with a
passion. He sees him as a modern Tamburlaine, a dy-
namic power-hero immune to the flatness of everyday

life. (Actually, Blenholt was a diabetic crook who died
because he was addicted to candy.) While Max tries
to get Coblenz and Munves to go to the funeral, Ruth
tries to get Max to go to the Miramar—a neat seesaw
for Fuchs to play on. In spite of Max's desperate efforts,
neither Coblenz nor Munves goes. (Munves is hooked
on an etymological find: Sealwudu has been mistakenly placed in Essex by Krapp, the grand old man of
etymology. Coblenz's toothache has wedded him to the
bottle; he beats a broom futilely against the ceiling of
his apartment.) There is a little pearl peddler who
wanders in and out of the tenement, trying to unload
a string of fake pearls. They suggest Old Miller's dia-
monds in the earlier novel. But it is in the character
of the father that we see most clearly what a large
step Fuchs has taken between his first and second
novels. Label Hayman, the passive schlemiel of *Summer in Williamsburg,* is now Max Balkan's father, an
ex-tragedian of the Yiddish theater; he works as a
sandwich man, advertising Madame Clara's scientific
beauty treatments, and he sits around the apartment
in a clown's costume, reading the *Tag.* And what a
difference that costume makes! Just as Cohen, the
writer, has been intensified in Munves, the etymologist,
and Philip, the dreamer, in Max, the dreamer-on-the-
make, so the realistic Label Hayman has become the
symbolically richer Mr. Balkan.

Homage to Blenholt, one might say, is *Summer in
Williamsburg* rewritten from a point of view. The
noose of action is pulled tighter, the phantasy is given
freer rein, the absurdity is wilder on the surface but
more controlled at the root. The humor is now implicit

in the structure of the novel, not incidental to it. The funeral scene has the madness of a debacle in grand opera in which nothing comes off. Max, an underprivileged Hamlet, acts at last. He tries to rescue an enraged woman who dashes up to the rostrum at the funeral service; her car, which tied up the funeral procession, has had the air let out of its tires by Blenholt's gangster cronies. For his trouble, Max is trampled by the crowd and is offered one of the funeral cars by a gangster as a place in which to recuperate. He finally makes it home, shaken and sadder, but only slightly wiser. For when he gets there, he finds that he has received a nibble from Onagonda Onion Products, Incorporated, who are interested in his idea of bottling onion juice. The news of his luck races through the tenement; the mirage of success shimmers. Max is rewarded, in the end, with a five-pound bag of onions. Munves marries Max's sister Rita—a marriage made possible, ironically, by Coblenz's winnings on the horses—and Ruth finally drags Max off to see Joan Crawford at the Miramar. Mr. Balkan, the clown, sums up in a serious coda:

> Then he knew what it was that had been troubling him vaguely before. In his wife's earthly guffaws he recognized the clamorous demands of the world, its insistent calls for resignation and surrender, and he knew now that Max would never be the same again. Much had gone out of Max, aspiration, hope, life. His son would grow old and aging, die, but actually Max was dead already for now he would live for bread alone. That was the rule and few men were strong enough to disobey

it. It had happened to Mr. Balkan himself, he knew, and now it had happened to his son. And regretting the way of the world, Mr. Balkan realized that he had witnessed the exact point at which his son had changed from youth to resigned age. Walking out of the house and shifting the shoulder straps to get the signs comfortably settled, it seemed to the old man that this death of youth was among the greatest tragedies in experience and that all the tears in America were not enough to bewail it.

But all the same the evening sun that day went down on time.

In *Homage to Blenholt,* Fuchs found the ideal way of using his material. Starting out as a social realist, saturated in his subject but with no way of commenting on it, he evolved into a satirist. Because satire not only heightens reality but criticizes it, Fuchs was able to transfigure reality without making it overtly symbolic. Max's inventions are subtle mockeries of the myth of the self-made man; the portrait of Munves rings changes on the plight of the intellectual in America; and Coblenz, the horseplayer, offers us an unconscious parody of the great adult game of the American economy, the stock market. Mr. Balkan receives wave lengths from two directions: the realism of Label Hayman, and the larger-than-life exaggerations of the movies. Combining the best features of both, he becomes theatrical without becoming fake. And by making Blenholt the commissioner of sewers, the most human of all utilities, Fuchs takes advantage of the most powerful fulcrum of satire—the turning of physical necessity into social absurdity. Where *Summer in Williamsburg* is a truthful description of reality, *Homage to Blenholt* is the real thing, a creation.

Low Company differs from either. It has a depth of perception not found in the other novels. It is, technically speaking, the most accomplished—in plotting, character development, and objectification. It is admirable but imperfect. The scene switches from Williamsburg to Neptune Beach (Brighton Beach). Mr. Spitzbergen, a candy store owner, has rented some of the slums he owns to Shubunka, a fat, crippled, effete crook, who uses them as brothels. A crisis results when a brothel-owning syndicate muscles in on Shubunka. There are two adroit surprises in the handling of the plot: Spitzbergen is murdered instead of Shubunka, and he is murdered not by the syndicate but by Moe Karty, a desperate horseplayer being hounded for money. The humor is no longer satiric but sardonic. *Low Company* is a savage book. Fuchs lays bare the grinning skeleton of the petty-bourgeois world. He knows Spitzbergen inside out; one of the troubles is, we do, too. (This was probably not true in the thirties; since then the sinister little merchant, congealed in his own moral values, has been gone over with a fine-tooth comb.) Shubunka is the real invention here: ugly, narcissistic, cunning, and peculiarly sympathetic. He is another misfit mad for communication and affection. And there are two minor characters as good as they come: Shorty, a swaggering, prurient soda jerk, and Madame Pavlovna, a corsetière as ruthless as she is fruity. The scene in which Shorty tries to seduce

her is not only hair-raising but chillingly funny. It is
comic in the way a George Grosz cartoon is comic:
we recognize the victims, we are aware of the appropri-
ateness of the depiction, and we are frightened.

Low Company has the nervous rhythms and drive
of a good thriller, and a passion the other books lack.
But Fuchs makes a serious mistake in *Low Company*.
He has learned how to tell a story and he has objectified; he has objectified too far for Fuchs. In place
of the intellectual dreamers—Philip, Max, Cohen,
Munves—with whom he has a natural identification
and sympathy, we have, as the author's stand-in, Lurie,
the owner of a dress store, who is in love with one of
Spitzbergen's cashiers. Lurie is the merely good and
ordinary man. And, unlike the dreamers, he can act.
He bears the moral weight of the novel, and it is crush-
ing. The choice of Lurie as a hero leads Fuchs to the
one false psychological passage in a thousand pages:

> Going up the hallway, deep in reflection, Lurie
> found that the mood of despondency which had
> oppressed him all day had suddenly lifted. Per-
> haps this was because of his quarrel with Dorothy
> and the end to plans of marriage, but his strange
> easy-heartedness, it seemed to him, went beyond
> the relief here. For once now he felt satisfied and
> resolved. His old inner distaste for Neptune Beach
> and the people there had gone. Witnessing the res-
> ignation of Shubunka as the man walked to the
> subway, realizing that he, too, had conscience and
> recognized in his own peculiar way the justice of
> his fate, above all, feeling with pity his complete
> wretchedness, Lurie knew now that it had been
> insensible and inhuman for him, too, simply to

hate Neptune and seek escape from it. This also was hard and ignorant, lacking human compassion. He had known the people at Ann's in their lowness and had been repelled by them, but now it seemed to him that he understood how their evil appeared in their impoverished dingy lives and, further, how miserable their own evil rendered them. It was not enough to call them low and pass on.

This is not only hurried but unconvincing. We are back to the cardboard moral resolution of the novel of social realism—and in a novel that otherwise can make some claim to perfection. In *Summer in Williamsburg,* the characters are real; in *Homage to Blenholt,* they are significant by implication; and in *Low Company,* they are both—except for Lurie. Some personal impetus has been lost by the writer in regard to one character, a character that so much depends on. What Lurie needs is the authority of a character such as Gatsby, who exists convincingly in the world of his novel and achieves a dimension by inference outside it. Lurie is not important; Fuchs tries to make him important. Our interest remains focused on Shubunka.

Fuchs, who has been writing for the movies since the early forties, is that rare bird, a writer both witty and loving. He is free of malice at one end of the spectrum and free of sentimentality at the other. At a time when no one had a viewpoint and everyone took a stand, Fuchs was talented and intelligent enough to be an exception. His three novels, buried in the thirties, rise up in the sixties and shine.

[1961]

Katherine Anne Porter
No Safe Harbor

Katherine Anne Porter's *Ship of Fools* is the story of a voyage—a voyage that seems to take place in many dimensions. A novel of character rather than of action, it has as its main purpose a study of the German ethos shortly before Hitler's coming to power in Germany. That political fact hangs as a threat over the entire work, and the novel does not end so much as succumb to a historical truth. But it is more than a political novel. *Ship of Fools* is also a human comedy and a moral allegory. Since its author commits herself to nothing but its top layer and yet allows for plunges into all sorts of undercurrents, it is disingenuous to read on its surface alone and dangerous to read for its depths.

Except for the embarkation at Veracruz and a few stopovers at ports, all the events occur aboard the *Vera,* a German passenger freighter, on its twenty-seven-day journey from Mexico to Germany in the summer of 1931. There is no lack of passengers; the cast is so immense that we are provided with not one but two keys at the beginning, so that we can keep the characters clearly in mind. The passenger list includes many Germans; a remarkable company of Spanish zarzuela singers and dancers—four men and four women—equally adept at performing, thieving, pimping, and whoring; the satanic six-year-old twins of two of the dancers; and four Americans—William Denny, a know-nothing chemical engineer from Texas; Mrs. Treadwell, a divorcée in her forties, who is constantly thwarted in her attempts to disengage herself from the rest of the human race; and David Scott and Jenny Brown, two young painters who have been having an unhappy love affair for years, have never married, and quarrel endlessly. There are also a Swede, some Mexicans, a Swiss innkeeper and his family, and some Cubans. The Germans are almost uniformly disagreeable—an arrogant widow, a windbag of a professor named Hutten, a violently anti-Semitic publisher named Reiber, a drunken lawyer, an Orthodox Jew who loathes Gentiles, a dying religious healer, and a hunchback, to name just a few. Each suffers from a mortal form of despair—spiritual, emotional, or religious. At Havana, La Condesa, a Spanish noblewoman who is being deported by the Cuban government, embarks, and so do eight hundred and seventy-six migrant workers, in steerage. They are being sent back to Spain because of the collapse of the Cuban sugar market.

In the little world of the *Vera,* plying across the ocean, the passengers become involved with one another not from choice but by proximity. Because of this, not very much happens, from the viewpoint of conventional drama. Miss Porter is interested in the interplay of character and not in the strategy of plotting. Her method is panoramic—cabin to cabin, deck to writing room, bridge to bar. She has helped herself to a device useful to a natural short-story writer: she manipulates one microcosm after another of her huge cast in short, swift scenes. Observed from the outside, analyzed from within, her characters are handled episodically. Place is her organizing element, time the propelling agent of her action. The *Vera* is a Hotel Universe always in motion.

As it proceeds, small crises blossom into odious flowers and expire. There are three major events. An oilman, Herr Freytag, a stainless Aryan, is refused the captain's table once it is learned that the wife he is going back to fetch from Germany is Jewish. A woodcarver in steerage jumps overboard to save a dog thrown into the sea by the twins and is drowned. And the zarzuela company arranges a costume party "gala" whose expressed purpose is to honor the captain but whose real motive is the fleecing of the other passengers. The characters, seeking release or support in one another, merely deepen each other's frustrations. Often these random associations end in violence—a violence always out of character and always revealing. Hansen, the Swede, who talks about a society in which the masses are not exploited, clubs the publisher with a beer bottle. The source of his immediate anger is his disappointed passion for one of the Spanish dancers. The funeral of the wood-carver, the gentlest of men, becomes the occasion for a religious riot. Mrs. Treadwell, a carefully contained woman, well aware of the pointlessness and danger of meddling in other people's business, emerges from behind her bastion and beats up Denny in a drunken frenzy with the heel of a golden evening slipper.

If the relationships are not violent, they are damaging. Schumann, the ship's doctor, falling suddenly in love with the drug-addicted and possibly mad Condesa, risks his professional, spiritual, and emotional identity. The American painters hopelessly batter themselves in an affair they cannot resolve or leave alone. And the most solid of Hausfraus, Professor Hutten's wife, speaks up suddenly, as if against her will, to contradict her husband at the captain's table, an act doubly shameful for being public. Unable momentarily to put up with her husband's platitudes, to support a view of marriage she knows to be false, Frau Hutten, in her one moment of insight, undermines the only security she has. As character after character gives way to a compulsion he has been unaware of, it becomes evident why Miss Porter's novel is open to many interpretations. Through sheer accuracy of observation rather than the desire to demonstrate abstract ideas, she has hit upon a major theme: order versus need, a theme observable in the interchange of everyday life and susceptible of any number of readings—political, social, religious, and psychological. Every major character is magnetized in time by the opposing forces of need and order. Mexico is the incarnation of need, Germany the representative of an order based on need. At the beginning, in Veracruz, there is a hideously crippled Mexican beggar, "dumb, half blind," who walks like an animal "following the trail of a smell." And the very

last character in the book is a German boy in the ship's
band, "who looked as if he had never had enough to
eat in his life, nor a kind word from anybody," who
"did not know what he was going to do next" and
who "stared with blinded eyes." As the *Vera* puts in
to Bremerhaven, he stands, "his mouth quivering
while he shook the spit out of his trumpet, repeating
to himself just above a whisper, 'Grüss Gott, Grüss
Gott,' as if the town were a human being, a good and
dear trusted friend who had come a long way to welcome him." Aboard the *Vera,* there is, on the one
hand, the captain's psychotic authoritarianism, with its
absolute and rigid standards of behavior, menaced always by human complexity and squalor; on the other,
the Condesa's drug addiction and compulsion to seduce young men. Both are terrifying forms of fanaticism, and they complement each other in their implicit
violence.

Dr. Schumann is the mediating agent between these
two kinds of fanaticism. Suffering from a weak heart,
he is going back to Germany—a Germany that no
longer exists—to die. He is the product of a noble Teu-
tonic strain, the Germany of intellectual freedom,
scientific dispassion, and religious piety. He is a healer
equally at home in the chaos of the steerage and in
the captain's stateroom. But the Condesa shatters his
philosophic detachment. He goes to her cabin at night
and kisses her while she is asleep; he orders six young
Cuban medical students to stay away from her cabin
because he is jealous. Both acts are symptoms of a
progressive desperation. First he refuses to express his
need openly, out of fear; then he masks it by a display

of authority. He becomes, finally, a conspirator in the Condesa's addiction. Since he is not able to separate the woman from the patient, in Dr. Schumann need and order become muddled. Mrs. Treadwell, an essentially sympathetic character, is drawn into Freytag's dilemma the same way—casually, then desperately. It is she who innocently tells her anti-Semitic cabinmate that Freytag's wife is Jewish, not knowing the information is meant to be confidential. Freytag is bitter, forgetting that he has already blurted out the fact at the captain's table in a fit of anger and pride. Mrs. Treadwell wisely points out that his secret should never have been one in the first place. This is odd wisdom; Mrs. Treadwell has a few secrets of her own.

It is from such moral complications that the texture of *Ship of Fools* evolves—a series of mishaps in which both intention and the lack of intention become disasters. The tragedy is that even the best motive is adulterated when translated into action. Need turns people into fools, order turns them into monsters. The *Vera*'s first-class passengers stroll on deck gazing down into the abysmal pit of the steerage—pure need—just as they watch in envy the frozen etiquette of the captain's table and its frieze of simulated order. Even dowdy Frau Schmitt, a timid ex-teacher who cannot bear suffering in others, finally accepts the cruelty of Freytag's dismissal from the captain's table. If she does not belong there herself, she thinks, then where does she belong? A victim, she thus becomes a party to victimization—a situation that is to receive its perfect demonstration in the world of Nazi Germany, which shadows Miss Porter's book like a bird of carrion. Through the need to belong, the whole damaging human complex of fear, pride, and greed, a governing idea emerges from *Ship of Fools* that is rooted in the Prussian mystique of "blood and iron." It is the manipulation of human needs to conform to a version of order.

The flow of events in *Ship of Fools* is based on addiction (sex, drugs, food, and drink) or obsession (envy, pride, covetousness, and the rest). Yet even the most despicable characters, such as the Jew-hating Herr Rieber, seem surprisingly innocent. It is the innocence of ignorance, not of moral goodness. The humbug and misinformation exchanged between the passengers on the *Vera* are voluminous. Each person is trapped in that tiny segment of reality he calls his own, which he thinks about, and talks about, and tries to project to a listener equally obsessed. Not knowing who they are, these marathon talkers do not know the world they are capable of generating. Love is the sacrificial lamb of their delusions, and though it is pursued without pause, it is always a semblance, never a reality. Though they are terribly in need of some human connection, their humanity itself is in question.

Only the Spanish dancers seem to escape this fate. They transform need into a kind of order by subordinating it for financial gain or sexual pleasure, without involvement. They are comically and tragically evil; they have arranged a universe of money around sex and fraud. Consciously malignant, they are outdone by the natural malice of the twins, who throw the Condesa's pearls overboard in a burst of demoniacal spirits. The pearls are a prize the Spanish dancers had planned to steal. The evil of design is defeated by natural evil—a neat point. Even in this closed, diabolical society, in which the emotions have been disciplined for profit, the irrational disturbs the arrangement of things.

At one point, Jenny Brown recalls something she saw from a bus window when she was passing through a small Indian village in Mexico:

Half a dozen Indians, men and women, were standing together quietly in the bare spot near one of the small houses, and they were watching something very intensely. As the bus rolled by, Jenny saw a man and a woman, some distance from the group, locked in a death battle. They swayed and staggered together in a strange embrace, as if they supported each other; but in the man's raised hand was a long knife, and the woman's breast and stomach were pierced. The blood ran down her body and over her thighs, her skirts were sticking to her legs with her own blood. She was beating him on the head with a jagged stone, and his features were veiled in rivulets of blood. They were silent, and their faces had taken on a saintlike patience in suffering, abstract, purified of rage and hatred in their one holy dedicated purpose to kill each other. Their flesh swayed together and clung, their left arms were wound about each other's bodies as if in love. Their weapons were raised again, but their heads lowered little by little, until the woman's head rested upon his breast and his head was on her shoulder, and holding thus, they both struck again.

It was a mere flash of vision, but in Jenny's memory it lived in an ample eternal day illuminated by a cruel sun.

This passage could be the center from which everything in Miss Porter's novel radiates. The human relations in it are nearly all reenacted counterparts of this silent struggle. Inside and out, the battle rages—the devout against the blasphemous, the Jew against the Gentile, class against class, nation against nation. The seemingly safe bourgeois marriages—of solid Germans, of stolid Swiss—are secret hand-to-hand combats. It is no better with lovers, children, and dogs. The dog thrown into the sea by the evil twins is at least rescued by the good wood-carver before he drowns. But on the human level the issues are obscure, the colors blurred; the saint is enmeshed with the devil. Struggling to get at the truth—*Vera* means "true" in Latin—the passengers in *Ship of Fools* justify its title. What truth is there for people who must lie in order to exist, Miss Porter seems to be asking. Against her insane captain and her mad Condesa, Miss Porter poses only the primitive and the remote—an enchanting Indian servant aboard ship, the appearance of three whales, a peasant woman nursing a baby. They are as affecting as a silence in nature.

Miss Porter is a moralist, but too good a writer to be one except by implication. Dogma in *Ship of Fools* is attached only to dogmatic characters. There is not an ounce of weighted sentiment in it. Its intelligence lies not in the profundity of its ideas but in the clarity of its viewpoint; we are impressed not by what Miss Porter says but by what she knows. Neither heartless nor merciful, she is tough. Her virtue is disinterestedness, her strength objectivity. Her style is free of displays of "sensitivity," musical effects, and interior decoration. Syntax is the only instrument she needs to construct an enviable prose. But the book differs from her extraordinary stories and novellas in that it lacks a particular magic she has attained so many times on a smaller scale. The missing ingredient is impulse. *Ship of Fools* was twenty years in the writing; the stories read as if they were composed at one sitting, and they have the spontaneity of a running stream. *Ship of Fools* is another kind of work—a summing up, not an overflowing—and it is devoid of one of the excitements of realistic fiction. The reader is never given that special satisfaction of the drama of design, in which the strings, having come unwound, are ultimately tied together in a knot. Miss Porter scorns patness and falseness, but by the very choice of her method she also lets go of suspense. She combines something of the intellectual strategy of Mann's *Magic Mountain* (in which the characters not only are themselves but represent ideas of human qualities) with the symbolic grandeur of *Moby Dick* (in which a predestined fate awaits the chief actors). Her goodbye to the themes of Mexico and Germany (two subjects that have occupied her elsewhere) is a stunning farewell, but it lacks two components usually considered essential to masterpieces—a hero and a heroic extravagance.

Ship of Fools is basically about love, a human emotion that teeters helplessly between need and order.

On the *Vera*'s voyage there is precious little of it. The love that comes too late for the Condesa and Dr. Schumann is the most touching thing in it. But the Condesa is deranged, ill, and exiled; the dying doctor is returning to a Germany that has vanished. The one true example of love—a pair of Mexican newlyweds—is never dwelt upon. We are left with this image of two people, hand in hand, who have hardly said a word in all the thousands that make up Miss Porter's novel. In *Ship of Fools,* every human need but one is exposed down to its nerve ends. Love alone remains silent, distant, and abstract.

[1962]

William Shakespeare
Mr. W. H. and
Mr. H. W.

In his preface to *William Shakespeare,* A. L. Rowse makes the following claim for his biography: "[My] approach to Shakespeare's life and work, and their relation to the age, has produced discoveries that have astonished me, shed light upon problems hitherto intractable, produced results which might seem incredible, if it were not for the consideration that this is the first time that an historian of the Elizabethan period has tackled them. . . ." Dr. Rowse modestly continues: "I am overwhelmed by what historical investigation, by proper historical method, has brought to light. It has enabled me to solve, for the first time, and definitively, the problem of the Sonnets. . . ."

Dr. Rowse knows a great many facts, and an historian, like anyone else, has the right to develop a thesis based on the facts he knows. But when he comes to prove that thesis—and Dr. Rowse is doing nothing less—he must produce those facts without prejudicing our judgment. What Dr. Rowse presents, instead, are merely assertions made with great heat, as if a rise in temperature could somehow transform suppositions into truths. And when we actually get down to documentation, it is often suspiciously shaky.

Dr. Rowse believes, for instance, that a speech in *A Midsummer Night's Dream,* taken by other authorities to refer to Queen Elizabeth, in reality refers to the third Earl of Southampton, Dr. Rowse's candidate for the patron-friend of the sonnets. In this speech, according to Dr. Rowse, Shakespeare is chiding the Earl to marry and beget children, a not unreasonable assumption since that is Shakespeare's theme in the first seventeen sonnets. The assumption is not unreasonable, however, *only* if we accept the dubious notion that characters in plays speak for their author, a notion which, in Shakespeare's case, would get us into immediate hot water.

The passage, as quoted by Dr. Rowse, follows:

To live a barren sister all your life,
Chanting faint hymns to the cold fruitless moon . . .
But earthlier happy is the rose distill'd,
Than that which withering on the virgin thorn
Grows, lives and dies, in single blessedness.

If we assume that the character is speaking for the author, and that the lines are relevant to Southampton, why are they addressed to a woman? Dr. Rowse goes on to say that the lines could not possibly relate to Elizabeth, to whom they would have constituted an insult. To believe this, we have to assume that every play Shakespeare wrote was precensored, with Elizabeth in mind. We also have to assume that a woman of Elizabeth's intelligence was so aesthetically naïve that she took every speech addressed to an unmarried female on the stage as a comment on herself.

But the three dots that follow line two are instructive. Dr. Rowse has omitted two lines between "moon" and "But earthlier happy is the rose distill'd." The two lines are:

> Thrice blessed they that master so their blood,
> To undergo such maiden pilgrimage;

Now it is true that "withering on the virgin thorn" is hardly complimentary to virgins, male or female. But wouldn't the inclusion of the two missing lines make it possible for the speech to have been said in front of Elizabeth? For aren't "they"—nuns, maidens, women in single state—"thrice blessed?" And wouldn't the inclusion of these two lines work against Dr. Rowse's thesis? Since he is generous in his use of quotations elsewhere, we may legitimately ask why the lines were omitted and whether his argument, in view of the passage as a whole, can stand the light of examination. Here, Dr. Rowse is fuzzy in the general by pretending that a work of art has the same factual force as a historical document, and fuzzy in the particular by arranging the evidence to suit his convenience.

Dr. Rowse assigns himself similarly embarrassing tasks: the turning of the "mortal moon" sonnet into a comment on the Lopez conspiracy rather than one on the death of Elizabeth, and proving "definitively" that Marlowe is the Rival Poet of the sonnets on grounds equally questionable.

The sonnets are at the heart of Dr. Rowse's biography. Before the sonnets can be discussed, some facts about them need to be known:

1) There are 154 sonnets in all.

2) Numbers 1 to 126 are written to a young man, the poet's patron and friend, numbers 1 to 17 urging him to marry and procreate.

3) Most of sonnets 127 to 154 are written to or refer to a Dark Lady, with whom the poet has had or is having a passionate affair, and with whom, presumably, the young man of the first 126 sonnets has also become involved.

4) A Rival Poet who is luring Shakespeare's patron away with some success appears in certain sonnets.

5) And in Thorpe's printing of the sonnets in 1609, there is the famous dedication to a "Mr. W.H., the onlie begetter of these insuing sonnets." (It would be wise to remember at the outset that this dedication appears in Thorpe's printing of Shakespeare's sonnets and is not necessarily Shakespeare's, and quite possibly Thorpe's. It is also theoretically possible for Thorpe to have transferred the dedication from Shakespeare's manuscript.)

The following questions, then, arise:

1) Who is the friend of sonnets 1 to 126?

2) Who is the Dark Lady?

3) Who is the Rival Poet?

4) Who is Mr. W.H.?

5) What are the dates of the sonnets?

And, in a recent book by Dover Wilson, *An Introduction to Shakespeare's Sonnets*—slyly subtitled *for Historians and Others*—a further question comes up:

6) Are the sonnets arranged in their proper sequence?

The young man would appear to be either Henry Wriothesely, the third Earl of Southampton (Rowse), or William Herbert, the third Earl of Pembroke (Wilson). These have been the two chief contenders ever since the "sonnet mystery" became a scholarly obsession.

Dr. Rowse is certain that even though the young man is Henry Wriothesely, the initials themselves stand not for him but for William Harvey, his stepfather, the third husband of the Earl's mother, the Countess of Southampton. According to this theory—which precludes the possibility of the dedication's originally having been Shakespeare's—it is Harvey who brought the sonnets to Thorpe to publish. Southamptonites have always had a difficult time explaining why Shakespeare would have reversed the initials for Henry Wriothesely. *They* claim that since the dedication is Thorpe's and the initials stand for William Harvey, there *is* no problem.

Why, then, does Thorpe describe Harvey as the "onlie begetter"? Dr. Rowse explains this, as follows:

There is no problem with the word "begetter," though it has misled generations: Shakespeare himself uses it in the sense of to get or acquire. Hamlet bids the players: "for in the very torrent, tempest, and, as I may say, whirlwind of your passion, you must acquire and beget a temperance that may give it smoothness. . . ."

Why quote Shakespeare as proof if the dedication is Thorpe's? And if *beget* means "acquire," why is Shakespeare redundant in the passage quoted from *Hamlet*? Wouldn't a more reasonable interpretation of the line suggest that there is a distinction in meaning between *acquire* and *beget*? And why would Thorpe call Harvey a getter or acquirer in the first place, since Harvey was in possession of the sonnets? The implication, I suppose, is that Harvey got them, at one time or another, from his wife, the Countess of Southampton, mother of the third Earl of Southampton, or openly or secretly from Southampton himself, and Thorpe is expressing his gratitude.

Now even if Dr. Rowse should turn out to be correct in some heavenly court of adjudication, how can the assumption, in view of the evidence supplied, be nailed down as fact? For certainly the word *beget* has another meaning equally possible to apply: to procreate, generate, or produce. It is not Dr. Rowse's being right or wrong that is so irritating—any reasonable idea is worth considering—but his insistence on absolute certainty in the face of contrary possibilities.

Dr. Wilson, on the other hand, makes an interesting case for the Dark Lady herself having brought the

sonnets to Thorpe, neither the poet nor the patron
wanting to see them in print because of their intimate
nature. The Dark Lady, it would seem, was a person
of less delicate sensibilities. Pembrokeites more or less
ascribe to the idea that the dedication, though Thorpe's,
must have originally been Shakespeare's, that the dedication was already inscribed on the manuscript brought
to Thorpe by the Dark Lady.

Both Earls were young (taking into account the varying dates assigned to the sonnets by Dr. Rowse and Dr.
Wilson), rich, handsome, and prominent. Each refused
to marry the eligible girl chosen for him (which explains, perhaps, the tone of the first seventeen sonnets),
and each was a patron of the arts. On the Southampton
side, there is no question of his having been Shakespeare's patron at one time, for both "Venus and
Adonis" and "The Rape of Lucrece" were dedicated
to him by Shakespeare. On the Pembroke side, assum-
ing that the dedication of the sonnets is relevant—and
it is to Dr. Wilson's credit that he is not sure—we can
start with a simple-minded fact in Pembroke's favor:
the initials "W.H.," standing for William Herbert,
come in the right order.

The identity of the Dark Lady is almost universally
admitted to be unknown and unknowable, though a
Negro courtesan of the period has been suggested for
the role by one scholar. (Scholars can be very literal.)
The Rival Poet has been narrowed down, over the centuries, to either Marlowe or Chapman. Marlowe is
Rowse's man, Chapman is Wilson's. The dates of the
sonnets—upon which so much depends—are hotly con-
tested. Dr. Rowse thinks they were written as early as

1592–1593, Dr. Wilson much later, starting in 1598 or 1599 and running through the early years of the seventeenth century.

Behind these specific dilemmas, there is a general ambiguity: how homosexual, if at all, are the sonnets? There would seem to be no real evidence whatever—letters, gossip, references in Shakespeare's work, hints and glimmers in the work of his contemporaries—linking Shakespeare to homosexuality. (This is not true of Southampton who, in later life, became visibly fond of his corporal general, according to Dr. Rowse.)

It is the tone of the sonnets, not factual clues, that bring the matter up in the first place, and since that tone allows for no assurances, there are no assurances to be had. Dr. Wilson goes into the matter thoroughly and presents cogent reasons that would militate against a serious view of Shakespeare as a homosexual: the existence and nature of the sonnets to the Dark Lady, the tone—at least in the early sonnets—of paternal or avuncular concern in regard to the young man, and the lack of any mention of a celebrated liaison between two men, a striking fact in view of how often Shakespeare mined the Greek and Roman worlds for material.

In sonnet 20, Shakespeare makes an explicit distinction between the poet's feelings for the young man and sexual desire:

And for a woman were thou first created;
Till Nature, as she wrought thee, fell a-doting,
And by addition me of thee defeated,
By adding one thing to my purpose nothing.

But since she prick'd thee out for women's pleasure,
Mine be thy love, and thy love's use their treasure.

But Dr. Wilson cannot have it both ways, either. On page two of his book, he speaks of the sonnets "as the greatest love-poem in the language . . . the mystery of [whose] detail [is] so unimportant as to fade away." Bravo. On page forty, he says, in defending Shakespeare against the charge of flattering his patron for money, ". . . what an attentive reader hears is the voice . . . of an ardently affectionate uncle or guardian. . . ." Perhaps there is a tradition of great love poems written by uncles and guardians to their nephews. If so, I am unaware of it.

Dr. Wilson is saying, by and large, something far more important. These love poems transcend any particular experience or version of love; they are supreme works of art having universal human relevance. What he does not quite say is that they also transcend the tangled histories that have been woven around them. Both Dr. Rowse and Dr. Wilson seem to agree that the sonnets offer no reasonable ground for suspecting Shakespeare of homosexuality. It is odd, therefore, to find them using the sonnets, in other connections, as offering reasonable ground. If the facts of Shakespeare's sexual life remain obscure in "the greatest love-poem in the language," how can we be sure of other facts to be found in the same text? Obviously we can't, one proof of which being that Dr. Rowse and Dr. Wilson do not agree on any of the important facts involved.

Dr. Wilson's book is economical, closely reasoned, and abjures the dogmatic certainty that gets Dr. Rowse into so much trouble. Still, one might say to Dr. Wilson that sonnets are poems, not evidence. Is his introduction, impeccably scholarly as it is, the proper one to

preface "the greatest love-poem in the language"? And
to Dr. Rowse, one might say what would seem obvious:
literature is not history. There is very little sense in
either of these books of Shakespeare as a *writer*. Read
consecutively, these two absolutely contradictory works,
written to establish what facts can be known about
Shakespeare's sonnets, leave the matter exactly where
it was before they were published.

[1963]

John Keats
The Noose
of the Whole

The *John Keats* of Walter Jackson Bate is a biography in only the conventional sense, for it far outstrips our usual notion of what the written history of a life should be. As biography per se, it would be hard to conceive of a recording of events more accurate and detailed. Mr. Bate, a critical authority on Keats, seems to know Keats's life to the same degree that his protagonist experienced it—month by month, week by week and, sometimes, day by day.

The entire Keats story took place in the short span of twenty-six years. Our incredulity at what was packed into those few short years increases. As individual episodes we thought we knew expand in Mr. Bate's biography, the noose of the whole pulls tighter; the story becomes more depressing by nature of its compression. In no other writer was inner greatness, intelligence, and charm met by such a consistent outward display of adversity. An unusual capacity for simple happiness was thwarted at every turn by accident, poverty, disease, and malice. Keats was a strong man who struggled against circumstance, not a weak one who succumbed to it. He was only five feet and three-quarters of an inch tall, but his life takes on the heroic proportions of a giant done in by flies.

Mr. Bate skillfully takes us over familiar ground: the death of Keats's young parents; the attempt of the three Keats boys to construct some semblance of family life together, while Fanny Keats, the youngest child, was taken over by their guardian, Richard Abbey (under whose relentless surveillance she remained inaccessible to Keats most of the time). Also, the death of Tom Keats at the age of eighteen from tuberculosis; the emigration of George, the second brother, to the wilds of Kentucky; the vicious and snobbish attacks on Keats's work; the disastrous love affair with Fanny Brawne; the nightmares of disease, the exile to Rome, and death.

The author is especially informative on the last days in Rome. Severn, the painter—who in accompanying Keats to Rome makes his one claim to immortality—was a tireless, devoted, inefficient, and complaining friend to the end. It is a measure of Mr. Bate's ability and fairness that he can examine Severn in these several lights without diminishing the force of Severn's loyalty to Keats.

Mr. Bate is equally well informed on every major and minor character in Keats's life, and he redresses the distortions of literary legend through a calm and systematic application of fact. In particular, he rescues Fanny Brawne from two simple-minded but contrasting views of her that have come to be prevalent: the mindless flirt and the maligned saint. And he makes it clear that Leigh Hunt was not, as he is so often depicted, a completely frivolous man. Fanny Brawne was intelligent and Leigh Hunt was kind. If neither of them was as kind or as intelligent as Keats, that is to be expected: Fanny Brawne was not a great person and Hunt was not a genius.

The author brings perspective and understanding to bear on everyone concerned without being sentimental in the process. He is not merely out to redress wrongs. Abbey, for instance, who lied to the Keats children about their inheritance and juggled their incomes to his own advantage, remains what he has always been, a petty crook. Mr. Bate's objectivity is easily proved. Obviously devoted to Keats, he is more impartial to Hunt than Keats himself. We never have, in reading this biography, the slightly uncomfortable feeling that a little more or a little less than the truth is being told.

Several ambiguities come a shade closer to full light. Though the last years of Keats's mother's life remain clouded in mystery, her power as a person and her early death seem to have made a greater impression on him than is even usual. Keats rarely mentioned her again; his silence could hardly be attributable to indifference. And in his attitude and relations to women, he often felt uncomfortable and hostile, particularly in the company of the sisters of his close friend, John Reynolds. Keats disliked the small talk of women, but his aversion possibly had deeper psychological undertones.

The paranoid turn that the letters to Fanny Brawne take at the end was less based on reasonable jealousy —if jealousy is ever reasonable—than on a conflict within Keats himself. The intensity of his work was threatened by the intensity of his feelings for Fanny. He wanted to end his anxiety either by possessing her completely or by ridding himself of her entirely. Unconsciously seeing her as a mirror of his emotions, she became the guilty vehicle of his own uneasiness.

Tracing the outlines of the narrative and filling in its corners is not the chief virtue of Mr. Bate's book. Profoundly understanding Keats's temperament and mind, his grasp of the philosophical abstractions that concerned Keats is extraordinary. The nature and quality of Keats's letters make him, in a sense, his own commentator. Mr. Bate, like Keats, is able to ground these abstractions in the specific, but he has the advantage of seeing the life, poems, and letters as a whole. The cogency of his explication of the complicated ins and outs of Keats's thought illuminates what has only been dimly understood before. We can, at last, witness the full transition of Keats the schoolboy into Keats the great writer. Unbelievably, that transition took three years, and the greatest poems were written in the space of a few months.

Keats began as a naïve and sentimental poet, writing in the fashion of his day—a fashion best exemplified in the work of Leigh Hunt. Through Benjamin Robert Haydon, a painter, he became aware of the limitations of Hunt. (Later, he became aware of the limitations of Haydon.) His problem as an artist—and Mr. Bate contends it is the major problem of every poet since Milton—was how to achieve the epic greatness of the major English poets without relinquishing the romantic focus on individual sensibility or repeating what had already been done before. This concern of Keats's was neither a matter of vanity or self-interest but the result of intelligence and acumen.

As unpetty as he was honest in his reactions, Keats saw the lack of power in the art around him. Bringing to literature a freshness and innocence that more sophisticated writers had long lost, he could not fail to see that the Elgin marbles were more important than Haydon's gigantic paintings, that Homer had written something Hunt could not emulate, that *King Lear* was wildly in contrast to the plays being produced at the Drury Lane. Such simple observations were at the heart of what later became a philosophic search, in which complex questions of art and life were ultimately tested.

The premium put on originality in poetry in Keats's time finally degenerated into decorative prettiness. Only Wordsworth among his contemporaries struck him as doing major work, and even Wordsworth, he felt, lacked amplitude. Keats, first embracing, then shunning the conventional styles of his day—both in literature and in literary society, which he came to loathe—tried to absorb the large preoccupations of Greek myth and the formal scope of the Elizabethan drama, Milton, and Dante.

Exhausting the constriction of the sonnet and the triviality of the song, Keats, ashamed of the vapidity of *Endymion*, grew conscious—perhaps fatally—of the way his thought outraced his work. He wanted to write a long, major poem. Unable to retreat to minor excellence, he could not quite move ahead to forge that combination he thought necessary—something of the introspective originality of Wordsworth at the service of the gigantic structures and themes of Shakespeare and Milton. The ultimate irony of Keats's life is that, tortured by a conception of greatness, he achieved it without recognizing it. Being original, it did not conform to what he thought greatness should be.

The conflict in Keats between the real and the ideal, his attempt to weld the opposing abstractions of indolence and action, joy and melancholy, beauty and truth are minor matters in a larger struggle between a poetry of individual consciousness (Wordsworth) and the "disinterestedness" of the great poets of the past (Shakespeare) who transcended individual consciousness. Keats may be the first modern writer, for he anticipated a dilemma that we see exemplified in Eliot's shift from poetry to the theater, in Joyce's use of Greek myth in *Ulysses,* in Mann turning to biblical sources for the Joseph novels, in Pound's reconstruction of history, and in Proust's fusion of Saint-Simon and the Arabian Nights.

A good case could be made out—Mr. Bate does not make it—for an unconscious solution of the problem in Keats's letters. They are important not only for their content, which is profound, but for their very existence as a separate body of literature. For better or worse, the greatness of the poet's mind is to be found in the letters, not in the poems, and the reach of thought he sometimes deplored as nonexistent in the poems is contained in those very letters that complain of the lack.

The story of his life has been told before. It has never been told more fully. The really remarkable thing about this work is Mr. Bate's complete understanding of Keats's development as a man, thinker, poet, and technician. He has the uncommon ability to hold these four difficult facets—each requiring, in turn, the specialized knowledge of the psychologist, the philosopher, the critic, and the prosodist—in genuine and simultaneous relation to each other. No complication of thought, no sudden shift of emotion, no intricacy in the construction and style of the poems is glossed over.

We do not see Keats as a lover, Keats mastering meter, Keats trying to discover the ultimate ends of poetry as isolated phenomena. Mr. Bate's book is free of that peculiarly false method of biography in which portraiture takes on the quality of piecework. What we have in this book, in short, is one of those rare and monumental studies in which a lifetime's devotion to an artist's life and work is finally distilled.

[1963]

Anton Chekhov

The Desert

Everywhere

Chekhov is not labeled a "critical" biography; one assumes, therefore, that Ernest J. Simmons merely set out to tell the story of Chekhov's life. A question immediately arises: how much of the life story of a great writer can you tell without dealing with his work? The answer—very little—instantly follows, and Mr. Simmons is aware of it. Second question: how far, then, do you have to go in dealing with it? Simmons starts out simply enough, confining himself to brief digests of the stories and the plays as they come into being. In the process of diligently quoting from Chekhov's letters—many of which, naturally, refer to Chekhov's work—he is slowly drawn into discussing Chekhov's discussions, and before you know it he has reached the thorny border of criticism. It is not a place where scholars plod lightly. As conscientious a historian as one could wish, and perhaps a little more so, Simmons is less satisfactory as an interpreter. His overall method is simple: dividing Chekhov's life into six distinct periods, he follows the outer circumstances of Chekhov's movements in each, makes educated guesses at his motivations (which demand the kind of education nobody has), and intersperses accounts of the stories and the plays.

If something of Chekhov the human being is absent from these carefully documented pages, the fault is only partly Simmons's. Writers alone, among biographical subjects, present a special problem. Barring a diary or two or the questionable memory of a contemporary (in this case, Lydia Avilova's gushy *Chekhov in My Life,* which Simmons demolishes), the incidents and characters available to the biographer are the very ones his subject has already transformed into literature. There is more to be learned, finally, about Chekhov's view of Lika Mizinova, a beautiful and intelligent girl he appeared to love but did not marry, from seeing *The Sea Gull* than there is from reading the letters he wrote her, just as there is more to be learned about the ancient Greeks from studying their myths than from finding out what they had for lunch.

The difficulties are compounded in Chekhov's case. Doctor and writer both, equally significant as a playwright and as a creator of fiction, he was as complicated personally as he was professionally. Of Olga Knipper, the actress he married three years before he died, Simmons says, "Olga's insight into her husband's enigmatic nature was at times extremely perceptive. With some truth she discerned that he really experienced no need to share himself and was inclined to look upon the daily lives of others quite indifferently." Simmons's statement is qualified; one would assume that *any* wife's insight into her husband's nature would with some truth be perceptive at times. Nevertheless, it is a strange statement to make about a man who when he was not writing was treating poverty-stricken patients and providing them with free drugs and medicines; traveling to Siberia (before the Trans-Siberian Railroad) to study the penal colonies on Sakhalin Island; building schoolhouses from his own plans and often with his own funds and labor; serving as a voluntary aide in famine relief and as a physician during epidemics of cholera; collecting books for the library of his native city; establishing a sanatorium in Yalta for impoverished victims of tuberculosis; commenting on the work of new young writers, which was sent to him by the bushel; serving as an unpaid census taker; and supporting, at various times and to varying degrees, a family of eight—himself, his four brothers, his sister, and his parents. Chekhov seemed to care a great deal about the daily lives of others. Yet it becomes clear in this biography that the warmth he showed toward innumerable contemporaries was checked by a paradoxical reserve that kept them from ever fully experiencing the intimacy they thought lay behind his friendliness. Chekhov knew more people than seems possible. When he was not engaged in the incredible exertion of his work—one mentions the nine hundred stories, the five superb full-length plays in passing— he managed, in the forty-four years of his life, to write over four thousand letters and to receive seven thousand. (Many, coming and going, are presumed lost.)

One of the busiest of men, Chekhov seems to have been one of the most accessible; in actuality, he was elusive. Giving more and more of himself away, he kept more and more of himself to himself. It is disconcerting to discover that someone as openhanded and gregarious as Chekhov—who said, "I positively cannot live without guests. When I'm alone, for some reason I become terrified"—should have had, several fathoms below the surface, the same resistance to human disruption one finds in Proust and Joyce. More than most authors, Chekhov gives us the impression of not being one, of simply observing life and writing it down. It was an impression he paid for during his lifetime. Here are the circumstances under which Chekhov worked in 1883:

I write under the most wretched conditions. Before me my nonliterary work mercilessly whips my conscience. In a neighboring room howls the child of a relative who has just arrived. In another room Father reads aloud to Mother. . . . Someone has wound up the music-box and plays "La Belle Hélène." I want to scamper off to the country, but it is already one o'clock in the morning. For a writing man it would be hard to imagine a more wretched situation. My bed is occupied by a relative who conducts a conversation with me about medicine. "My daughter must have a pain in her stomach and that is why she cries." I have the misfortune to be a medical man and everyone thinks it necessary to "have a chat" with me about medicine. And when they are bored talking about medicine, they take up the subject of literature.

Chekhov was born in 1860 in Taganrog, a port on the Sea of Azov. Its affluence was confined to the social lives of Greek shipping merchants, who lent a faint glow of European culture to what was essentially a slum. In spite of a symphony orchestra, a theater, and imported opera, its streets were muddy and its thoroughfares mostly unilluminated. It was also not without a touch of the fantastic: "Town authorities regarded with insufferable complacency the kidnaping of pretty young girls, who were whisked off the streets into carriages, destined for Turkish harems."

Chekhov's father, the owner of a small grocery store, had a passion for religion that masked an addiction to music; he endowed his children with a love of art and a distaste for dogma. Neither piety nor music proved effective against financial failure. Bankrupt, the elder Chekhov gave up the struggle; to escape his creditors he hid on a train for Moscow. His two older sons—Alexander, a talented journalist-writer, and Nicholas, a painter and illustrator—had already migrated to the capital in rebellion against his well-meaning tyranny. The rest of the family followed, with the exception of Anton, who stayed behind to finish his schooling.

Living as a tutor with the family who had mulcted his own in a shady real-estate deal, Chekhov made ends meet as best he could. At sixteen, he exchanged one harness for another; the economic rigors of independence supplanted the domination of an insolvent father. Freedom matured Chekhov while hardship tempered him. The past presented few occasions for regret; the warmth of a close family circle, amateur theatricals, and occasional excursions into the country seem to have been the only compensations for a dismal childhood that Simmons sums up in one sentence: "Homework, play, and sleep were all sacrificed to choir rehearsals, performances, and incessant church attendance."

Born poor, growing up where he did, Chekhov knew at first hand the squalor of the peasant, the exploitation of the apprentice, and the petty values of the shopkeeper. The discrepancies between his father's piety and commercial practices were particularly galling. Taganrog had scope; little of it was lost on Chekhov. But social spectrums are not as immediate as pocketbooks; and money, the straitjacket of Chekhov's early years, became the overriding fact of his existence. Later a deadlier one—tuberculosis—was added. Chekhov fought the classical battles of the gifted, against poverty and disease, and a third, with which Russian talent was not usually burdened: unlike the well-born Tolstoy and Turgenev, Chekhov, whose grandfather was a freed serf, felt compelled to "squeeze the slave" out of himself "drop by drop," exorcising his grandfather's bondage and the less literal but equally humiliating economic slavery of his father. "A genius who emerged from a privy," Chekhov's epigrammatic self-description, was a thumbnail sketch more rooted in fact than in self-disparagement.

Chekhov left Taganrog at the age of nineteen to study medicine in Moscow. There, under the pseudonym Antosha Chekhonte, he began to publish in the humorous magazines of the day. Fly-by-night affairs, these magazines were grab bags of entertaining and often vulgar trivia. Chekhov contributed short pieces— "parody, anecdotes, jokes, aphorisms, satiric sketches, short stories, and dramatic scenes." N. A. Leikin, the editor of a Saint Petersburg weekly, *Fragments,* liked Chekhov's work, met him, and began to publish him. His reputation grew, but he remained unaware of the extent of it until his first visit to Saint Petersburg. Leikin, who had carefully concealed from Chekhov his growing fame, in fear of competition and in the hope of paying him as little as possible, persuaded Chekhov to do a bimonthly column, "Fragments of Moscow Life," and Chekhov became a bona fide journalist. Columnist, humorist, turning out short stories with the single aim of earning money, he did not take a literary career seriously. "I regard medicine as my lawful wife and literature as my mistress," he said. (Ironically, he was later to use the same metaphor in making a distinction between his fiction and his plays.) Chekhov, in his own words, "attempted everything except novels, poetry, and denunciations." Yet, in a letter to his brother Alexander, who was working on A. S. Suvorin's *New Times,* in Saint Petersburg, he wrote, "I'm a newspaperman because I write much, but this is temporary. I'll not die as one."

Suvorin, superseding Leikin as Chekhov's publisher, became one of his closest friends and the most important of his correspondents outside the family. Though they were widely divergent in their views—Suvorin's paper was reactionary and bribable, and it toadied to the regime—some human connection outweighed their ideological and personal differences. The Dreyfus case brought their incompatibility to a head, but there were attempts even then to smooth things over. Finally, the anti-Semitism, jingoism, and vicious personal attacks that characterized *New Times* ended the relationship. Suvorin played the valuable double role of confidant and literary mentor to Chekhov for many years, and Chekhov owed a great deal to his encouragement. But Chekhov outgrew Suvorin as he had outgrown Leikin. By the middle of the eighteen nineties, Chekhov, long divested of his pseudonym, had become the second most celebrated writer in Russia. (Tolstoy was still alive.)

The process is more fascinating from the social and literary points of view than from the emotional. Chekhov's charm and magnetism were remarkable, but in Simmons's book he appears as a solitary surrounded by crowds: Chekhov being reluctantly dragged on-stage to receive the plaudits of the crowd at the first performance of *The Cherry Orchard*; Chekhov receiving presents from the humble and the great on his last birthday and confessing to Stanislavsky that some simple fishing poles pleased him most; Chekhov fending off a kind of general love he needed to know existed but that he did not want to come too close. On his watch chain he wore a pendant inscribed, "For the lonely man, the desert is everywhere," and the desert cropped up, like a permanent traveling mirage, whether he was in Siberia, at his estate at Melikhovo, in Paris, or in Yalta.

Chekhov's life was a family chronicle, and it lacked the tortures of passion and the ironies of fame. He was attracted to women but not undone by them, and success came to him early. Chekhov's freedom was martyred to family devotion, and the members of his family, mesmerized by their dominant character, gave up a good deal of their independence and something of

their individuality as personalities as well. Chekhov
was gentle but centrifugal. He often claimed he would
have been happier living alone. Certainly he would
have been richer, and freer to travel. The urge to roam
became a compulsive necessity as he grew older.
Whether the need to escape from his family, the manic-
depressive phases that can accompany tuberculosis, or
a completely unknown factor caused his sudden and
frequent leave-takings is not clear. Masha, his sister,
never married, though opportunities presented themselves, and she devoted her life to his interests; Alexander became a kind of intelligence agent for him,
looking out for his affairs in Saint Petersburg; Misha,
his youngest brother, joined the staff of *New Times,*
which published Chekhov's stories and already em-
ployed Alexander. Alexander, a writer himself, had to
contend with the yoke of a famous name. Chekhov's
relatives had reason to find him phenomenal: two generations from serfdom, he was a celebrity and a gold
mine. He always lived at the center of a large circle of
people; at the hub, the adoring and difficult ingroup of
his immediate family made the wheel hum.

Chekhov was extremely reticent about his personal
life. His close, lifelong attachment to Masha and his
mother was threatened only three times. His romantic
friendship with Lika Mizinova never seems to have
been fulfilled. Chekhov held her off until she ran away
with a married man. *The Sea Gull* was revised several
times to make the correspondences to life less glaring.
Lydia Avilova, a married woman with three children,
wrote a book about her "secret" affair with Chekhov
and seems to have fabricated Chekhov's emotions, if

not her own, out of hysteria and whole cloth. In his late marriage to Olga Knipper, Chekhov found what he said he wanted, a wife "who, like the moon, will not appear in my sky every day." Olga, who was devoted to him, learned what it is like not to be a sun; writers of genius are not inclined to hanker after soulmates. Olga was forced to stay in Moscow or Saint Petersburg, rehearsing and acting with the Moscow Art Theater, often in a play of her husband's, while his lungs condemned him to the kinder climate of Yalta. Their separations were often painful, but the situation seems to have suited Chekhov, by and large. At the end, there was no question of their being apart. Olga was no longer an actress or a wife—the roles she played in *The Sea Gull* and *Uncle Vanya*—but a nurse.

Simmons says that Chekhov's "own literary beginnings were singularly uninfluenced by his reading. The initial efforts of no artist of Chekhov's future eminence ever so completely and directly emerged from the very stuff of life." Though the press he worked for was vile, it is not incongruous that Chekhov should have started out as a journalist; he was fascinated by the anecdotal, he had an ear for the colloquial, and a healthy respect for the hard fact. As a doctor, he knew the value of disinterested observation. In the stories and the plays, the surface aspects of realism are always accurate and concrete, the connection to life never merely formal or rhetorical. If he disliked artifice, dogma was repellent. A firm admirer of Tolstoy, he abandoned that part of Tolstoy that was doctrinal:

Tolstoyan philosophy . . . governed my life for a period of six or seven years. . . . Now something within me protests; prudence and justice tell me that in electricity and steam there is more love for man than in chastity and abstinence from meat. War is evil and the court system is evil, but it does not therefore follow that I must go around in bast shoes and sleep on the stove along with the worker and his wife.

Chekhov's independence of spirit had both human and literary consequences. It made it possible for him to have friends as disparate as Tolstoy the neo-Christian, Gorky the political rebel, and Suvorin the reactionary, but it left him in a vulnerable position. Understanding many viewpoints, he subscribed to none, and he did so at a time when political allegiance and a thoroughgoing moral interpretation of life were considered the hallmarks of the serious artist. Chekhov was badgered throughout his career for such a viewpoint—one he was incapable of taking. He was intensely socially conscious, but committed himself always to individual people and projects. Distrusting mass movements, he loathed despotism, and smelled out its equivalent in the very forces that often claimed to oppose it. When political courage was required, Chekhov was not afraid to act. Soon after Gorky's election to the Imperial Academy of Sciences was annulled for political reasons, Chekhov resigned from the academy.

Too keen an observer to see life from fixed battlements, Chekhov was never a spokesman for the big theme or the all-embracing theory, but though the gigantic summing up was not in his line, he nevertheless became a giant. Like Gulliver, he was too big to be seen all at once. When, in 1888, he won the Pushkin Prize for a volume of short stories, he received five hundred rubles instead of the customary thousand, and "the committee unanimously expressed its sincere regret that Chekhov failed to esteem his talent, wrote for the cheap press, and often hurried his work." There was some justification for the committee's strictures, according to Simmons. What the committee could not have known at the time was that, cumulatively, Chekhov's fiction would embody a vast Russian human comedy exempt from the limitations of nationalism; Chekhov's country, the no-man's-land where the abrasions of internal and external pressure meet, turned out in the end to be universal.

Simmons makes a distinction, echoing Chekhov's own, between the early, "objective" work and the later writing, which is "purposeful." Chekhov's development is a complicated business. It is hard to think of another writer whose work is at once so objective and so personal. Though Chekhov seems to want us to forget that a story is being *told,* we cannot forget the tone of his voice. His force as an artist derives from his being meticulously invisible but miraculously audible. What is now clear to us—a short-story writer needs a tone as much as he needs a subject—was not so clear at the time he was writing. How could it have been, since it is through Chekhov that we learned it? In fact, what seemed to be the defects of Chekhov—his inability to dramatize and to moralize, in any conventional sense

—turned out to be virtues that altered the future of the short story and the theater. ("Morals do not purify plays any more than flies purify the air," he said.) Though he never lost his sense of the anecdotal nature of the story, he was able to pierce through the crustaceous exterior of an event to the living creature inside. What enabled him to do so was a genius for psychological acuteness and an absolute control of tone—a subtle and unique blend of the melancholy, the farcical, and the ironic.

Two letters to Suvorin present clearly the two viewpoints of "objectivity" and "purpose." One is dated 1890:

> You scold me for objectivity, calling it indifference to good and evil, the absence of ideas and ideals, and so forth. . . . Of course, it would be pleasant to combine art with preaching, but for me personally, this is . . . almost impossible. . . . I must . . . speak and think as they [his characters] would and feel with their feelings; otherwise, if I introduce subjective notes, the characters will become indistinct.

The other is dated 1892:

> . . . the writers whom we dub immortal or just simply good and who intoxicate us have one very important trait in common: they are going somewhere and summon you to go there with them, and you feel, not with your mind but with your whole being, that they have a purpose . . . they have immediate aims—the abolition of serfdom, the liberation of their country, politics, beauty. . . .

Others have remote aims—God, life beyond the grave, the happiness of humanity, and so on. The best of them are realistic and paint life as it is, but since every line is saturated with a consciousness of purpose, as though it were a juice, you feel, in addition to life as it is, life as it should be.

In 1902, however, he said to a young writer, Tikhonov:

You say that you have wept over my plays. Yes, and not only you alone. But I did not write them for this purpose, it is Alekseev [Stanislavsky] who has made such crybabies of them. I desired something other. I only wished to tell people honestly: "Look at yourselves, see how badly and boringly you live!" The principal thing is that people should understand this, and when they do, they will surely create for themselves another and better life.

Tikhonov asked Chekhov about those who already understood. Chekhov replied, "Well, they will find the road without me."

Is telling people honestly how badly and boringly they live "objective" or "purposeful"? In "telling people" something, purpose is implicit; in telling them something "honestly," objectivity is required. Chekhov seems to be arguing not against objectivity but for an objectivity that will bring revelations in its wake. Not interested in photographic realism, and dead set against the explicit message, he transformed social and philosophical issues into psychological conflicts. The "wish for another and better life" exists in almost all his characters, the very characters who are living so "badly and boringly." He exploited the psychological distance that separates the lives his characters live from the lives they want to live. The incongruity of the wish and the fact became the pivot point on which the plays turned. Chekhov never abandoned the mirror he held up to nature; nature allowed for every possibility. Chekhov found no need for the strict limitations of the political beauty salon, moral plastic surgery, or a philosophical wig; what he did instead was to change the surfaces and depths of the reflecting glass. In doing so, he came upon the fruitful innovation that distinguishes his work, which Simmons summarizes cogently:

> . . . by concentrating on the inner substance of people, he wished to reveal them as they really exist and not as they appear to be in real life. And just as this kind of concentration would require a realism that stressed not the events of life but a character's inner reaction to them, so must it be articulated by a dialogue that would reflect inner rather than outer action.

In Chekhov's theater we see this notion in practice. Chekhov's plays are unique in belonging to the tradition of the drama and in standing apart from it. The idea that Chekhov could not construct a play—an idea that haunted him—was false. He said—and it might be Ibsen speaking—"If in the first act you hang a pistol on the wall, then in the last act it must be shot off." He meant it. The plays are superbly constructed, but the principle of construction is new. They are devised as interconnected short stories in which small crises, revealing the secret lives of the characters, rarely lead to a large one, and in which the seams sewing the stories together are obscured from the audience. Cumulative action is not as apparent in Chekhov's plays as it is in Ibsen's—Chekhov disliked Ibsen's work—because the accumulating tension constantly exhausts itself in tiny reliefs. This technical originality is in keeping with the general point of the plays. Both the tragedy and the comedy of life stem from the same source: life does not lead to large crises but peters out in small ones. No matter how large the implication, it is always focused through a powerful but small magnifying glass.

Invaluable as documentation, *Chekhov* has two great virtues—the inclusion of material that has only recently come to light in the Soviet Union, and is therefore unattainable elsewhere in English; and the placing of Chekhov's works in chronological order in relation to his life. Monumental in design, painstakingly researched, *Chekhov,* unfortunately, is negligently written. Simmons cannot resist the flat-footed frisson ("Young Misha's noisy excitement ran through the family like a current of electricity"), the graybeard comparison ("The sap of literary talent had already started to run"), and redundant unintelligibility ("But deep within him lodged an inherent artistic sense, which would insistently demand fulfillment in any exposure to writing").

Biographers of great writers cannot be expected, alas, to write as well as their subjects.

[1963]

The Theater,
The New, and
The Now:
A Letter

As a fellow member of the Playwrights' Unit, I read Mr. L.'s article on playwriting with great interest. I would like to make some comments on it:

1) A play—like any other form of writing—is no better and no worse than the talent that produces it. It is therefore hard for me to conceive of "content and form," as Mr. L. uses those words, as dated or unuseable. It is perfectly true that imitations of original work of any period are valueless, but great work in the theater does not date for the same reasons that great work in painting does not date. The notion that the theater is somehow exempt from being a form of literature, and therefore a form of art, seems to me to beg the question. Plays are not handed down in an oral tradition; they

are written down. They are words on paper. They may
be different from—they *are* different from—other forms
of literature. But they cannot escape the fate of being
written in words. They are not dance, mime, panto-
mime, spectacle, or ritual.

2) Technical changes or advances may occur, but
technical newness can conceal warmed-over soup and
talent can make anything new. Mr. L. despairs when a
curtain goes up and he is faced with a living room.
Yet Ionesco uses a living room for his own purposes—
namely to show up the tired convention of using living rooms. A living room, nevertheless, is used and
no one can say that it cannot be used again for some
other purpose we do not, now, foresee.

3) Contemporary experience would have to inform
any contemporary play, even if it were written in
blank verse, or the play would not be true. Blank verse
can be part of the experience of a contemporary man.
How and whether a writer chooses to use it would be
his problem. But the past is contemporary insofar as it
is experienced in the present. *Antony and Cleopatra*
was a contemporary play in Elizabethan times even
though its subjects were no longer contemporary. Is
Antony and Cleopatra a contemporary play-now? It
depends on how strictly one defines contemporary. I
would say yes on the theory that all great art is permanently contemporary. Mr. L. does not go into that
problem. Why do works of art, then, hundreds of years
old, remain relevant? Because of the biological con-
tinuity of human life which transcends national differences as well as differences in time.

4) Freud underscored the point by calling a psycho-

logical pattern he observed in an office in Vienna in the nineteenth century an "Oedipus complex," from the Greek play, written 2500 years earlier.

5) Freud's theories are less old-fashioned than Mr. L. pretends. The half-baked exploitation of them by simple-minded writers who use them as cartoon explanations of all phenomena is simply a distortion and a reduction. What I think *is* true is that a playwright who saw his characters from a psychoanalytical point of view would be limiting their choice of action and their interest. Jocasta didn't commit suicide because she was neurotic.

6) Mr. L. says that guilt has become meaningless because there are no longer any absolute moral standards. If guilt is meaningless as a moral concept (a highly debatable point), it is still meaningful as a psychological and philosophical one. For a playwright, it is not a question of absolute rights and wrongs but the feelings his characters may have about them—feelings of shame and humiliation, say. In Camus's *The Fall,* the hero finds himself at the end of the novel guilty because he does not feel guilt. How to act in the face of a lack of moral standards is itself a moral question. Existentialism is concerned with the very problem Mr. L. dismisses. It is a far more difficult and profound one than he suggests.

7) I agree with Mr. L. that a banal thesis play whose "message" is "Crime does not pay" is not worth our attention. But surely that doesn't mean that *Crime and Punishment* or *The Trial* are not worth our attention. It is not the subject of a work but how profoundly it investigates its subject that counts.

8) Aristotle did not mean by "an imitation of an action" the realistic duplication of an everyday act. He meant, I believe, a series of events, gestures, speeches, and movements directed toward a particular goal. One might say, for instance, that the "action" of *Oedipus Rex* is freeing the city of Thebes from plague. The word "action" is closer in meaning to "purpose" and the word "imitation" to "revelation and accomplishment." Neither has much to do with realism as we understand it.

9) Unlike Mr. L., I suspect the realistic novel and play may still have a great deal to say. Whether that's true or not, who would want to be limited to the realistic play alone, or to be deprived of its possibilities? Words like *realism, contemporary, new,* and so on, are just words until there is a work by which we can illustrate them. I saw no play this year at the Playwrights' Unit that seemed to me as good as *The Sea Gull, Volpone,* or *The Rivals.* And I don't mean that facetiously but seriously. I'm not suggesting that they be written again, though that would be no worse than seeing the works of tiny Becketts and teentsy Genets. But these plays exist, they can be read, and, from time to time, they can even be seen. Why should we settle for less? I agree with Mr. L. that new plays should be new. But I also think they should be good.

[1963]

Nathalie Sarraute
Make It Vague

Nathalie Sarraute is the chief critical intelligence of the *roman nouveau* or *"l'anti roman"* or "antinovel novel" in France. Not only is the name of the movement in question; the identity of its adherents remains uncertain. Roughly speaking, it would appear to include the novels of Mme. Sarraute, the work of Robbe-Grillet, Pinget, Sollera, and Claude Mauriac, and, if one crossed the Channel, perhaps Philip Toynbee in England. In the four essays that make up *The Age of Suspicion,* written between 1947 and 1956, Mme. Sarraute presents us with a little guidebook to "the method" or at least *her* "method."

It is a disconcerting book, for a great deal of what Mme. Sarraute has to say by way of incidental observation seems true; yet her judgments on individual writers are often harsh and obtuse, and her major thesis, repeated in one way or another in each of the essays, is questionable. It is clear that Mme. Sarraute wants to brush away the dead wood of the novel; what is less clear is what she would put in its place. This difficulty

—of seeing what one is against without knowing what one is for—has its origin in two peculiar facts. Mme. Sarraute's critical theories are not explications, appreciations, or analyses of masterpieces of antinovel fiction, but precede their hypothetical creation. And since she is a practicing novelist, we are never certain whether she is speaking for a group or a movement, or for herself. Are we to take Mme. Sarraute's novels as examples of what she thinks should follow on the heels of Balzac, Tolstoy, Joyce, and Proust? Mme. Sarraute would be too modest, in spite of often being too arrogant, to make such a claim for herself. Calmly telling us what fiction should be, she cannot show us one contemporary example she approves of wholeheartedly, though, in passing, she ambiguously salutes Camus's virtuosity in *The Stranger,* and has words of praise for Henry Green and Ivy Compton-Burnett, neither of whom is an antinovel novelist. Attacking the masterpieces of the past because they *are* of the past—she could hardly attack them because they are masterpieces—Mme. Sarraute is in the embarrassing position of demolishing a museum, only to find herself standing empty-handed in the midst of the rubble.

There is no question about what Mme. Sarraute is against. She is discarding both the traditional "behaviorist," or realistic novel, and the work of her predecessors who rose up against it. She is as "anti" Joyce and Proust as she is "anti" Balzac, formidable figures whom she often reduces to the stature of pygmies, a process that casts more suspicion on herself than the suspicion of her title casts on the novel. (Mme. Sarraute uses the word to mean the distrust shared by authors and read-

ers alike who no longer believe in either the truth of
what they are writing or reading, or in each other.)
Here, for instance, is Mme. Sarraute on Joyce and
Proust:

> All Joyce obtained from those dark depths ["the
> dark places of psychology"] was an uninterrupted
> flow of words. As for Proust, however doggedly
> he may have separated into minute fragments the
> intangible matter that he brought up from the
> subsoil of his characters, in the hope of extracting
> from it some indefinable, anonymous substance
> which would enter into the composition of all hu-
> manity, the reader has hardly closed the book
> before . . . all these particles begin to cling to one
> another and amalgamate into a coherent whole
> with clear outlines, in which the practiced eye of
> the reader immediately recognizes a rich man of
> the world in love with a kept woman, a prominent,
> awkward, gullible doctor, a parvenue bourgeoise or
> a snobbish "great lady," all of whom will soon take
> their places in the vast collection of fictitious char-
> acters that people his imaginary museum.
>
> What enormous pains to achieve results that,
> without contortions and without hairsplitting, are
> obtained, shall we say, by Hemingway.

Comment 1: To describe the stream-of-consciousness
passages in *Ulysses* or all of *Finnegans Wake* as merely
"an uninterrupted flow of words" is to evade the task
of the critic. After all, every book is an uninterrupted
flow of words.

Comment 2: Are the results obtained by Proust and Hemingway comparable because they were both interested in "portraying character"? If so, why not include Shakespeare and James and Chekhov and Lawrence? Here, Mme. Sarraute is muddying, not illuminating. Perhaps, unlike those of us who have read Proust in translation and Hemingway in the original, Mme. Sarraute has read Proust in the original and Hemingway in translation.

Comment 3: In regard to Proust: the reader's eye does not have to be practiced. Proust did not intend his characters to have coherent wholes with blurred outlines.

Comment 4: Since Mme. Sarraute allows herself such vagaries as "all humanity" and "some indefinable, anonymous substance," we cannot share her dismay at coherent wholes.

Mme. Sarraute, wisely, sees some of Proust's merits —of all the great writers under attack, she handles him most gingerly, knowing somewhere in the intangible matter of the subsoil of her character that she has a lion by the tail; but his work—and who would deny it?—is done. For Mme. Sarraute, the revolt against the tradition is as unusable as the tradition, the revolt having become the tradition. In fairness to Mme. Sarraute, she sees clearly that the revolt against tradition is endless, but she makes no clear distinction between tradition and technique. The interior monologue, along with plotting, the delineation of character, "action," and so on are all false trappings, or used-up conventions, or both. The novelist's task is to "discover the new," his worst crime "repeating the discoveries of his predecessors." One would be hard put to quarrel with so general a proposition.

But even in stating it, one becomes uncomfortably aware of its scientific flavor. Literature is a kind of relay race of methodologies, in which advances occur, in which eventual improvements in technique will allow us, ultimately, to get at the heart of the matter. Which is what? Here, Mme. Sarraute becomes vague. The flux or tropisms or underground movements or interior wave-washes that make up universal psychological life—presumably that "indefinable, anonymous substance which would enter into the composition of all humanity."

But isn't it the novelist's business, not to mention the critic's, to define that substance? And in defining it, it can no longer be either indefinable or anonymous. What *is* this substance? In a passage of remarkable condescension, Mme. Sarraute says of Virginia Woolf: "Who today would dream of taking seriously, or even reading, the articles that Virginia Woolf wrote, shortly after the First World War, on the art of the novel?" (Comment: One would have to read the articles before one took them seriously.) Mrs. Woolf wanted to examine, naïvely, it seems, the "dark places" of the human psyche. It turns out, in the end, that that is more or less what Mme. Sarraute herself is after. If she has something else in mind, her style needs infinite refinement. There is behind Mme. Sarraute's argument, in spite of her intelligence and subtlety, a commitment to the notion that the values of progress are positive. When Mme. Sarraute starts smacking her lips over something "new"—Ivy Compton-Burnett's simultaneous use of conversation and subconversation in which only dialogue reveals the play of thought and the existence of event—we are unfortunately reminded of Mme. Curie in some Warner Brothers epic bending over her spirit lamp, about to convey to an anxious mate her discovery of radium. Mme. Sarraute, in short, is an academic in reverse; she is dogmatically prejudiced in favor of the new. She detests the contrivances of fiction she believes are taken for granted, the parceling out of description, psychology, and dialogue as if they were three different tubes of paint that reality could be conveniently squeezed into and out of. For her, the only legitimate character is "I," the only true work of the novel the luring of the reader into strange and difficult depths. The problem is: there have to be depths for the reader to be lured into.

Mme. Sarraute is most rewarding in her first chapter, "From Dostoievski to Kafka." Dostoievski, the supreme practitioner of the "psychological novel" and Kafka, the master of the novel "in situation," are not at opposite poles. Kafka's semi-anonymous *homo absurdus,* a twentieth-century hero, is the legitimate heir of Dostoievski's tragic clowns. The seemingly inconsistent advances and recoils of Dostoievski's characters represent to her a true image of the workings of a universal psyche:

> . . . these movements upon which all his [Dostoievski's] attention . . . [is] concentrated; which derive from a common source, and despite the envelopes separating them from one another, like

little drops of mercury, continually tend to conglomerate and mingle with the common mass; these roving states which, from one character to another, traverse the entire oeuvre, are to be found in everybody, refracted in each one of us according to a different index. . . .

The tie between this work . . . and the work of Kafka, to which people tend to contrast it today, appears evident . . . it [is] from Dostoievski's hands, more certainly than from those of any other, that Kafka . . . has seized the token.

Because these tenuous states are choreographed by Dostoievski in endless, magnetic gestures of attraction and repulsion, and because the states themselves are universal "psychological loam," Mme. Sarraute sees his characters, who cannot love but cannot exist in isolation, as props that envelop those states and express them. In Kafka's use of the character as prop she finds his identification with Dostoievski, and a sign of Kafka's mastery of the "underground" novel. In Kafka, where the names of the leading characters are reduced to initial letters, where the human contact so desperately sought by Dostoievski's characters is taken for granted from the beginning as impossible, the Dostoievskian movements are detached, desiccated, and crippled. Kafka is a psychologist by omission. Though we see the busy apparatus of the psyche heaving itself into motion in the few emotional contacts Kafka's novels provide, by describing the nonhuman world we live in he defines a human world by default. If I understand Mme. Sarraute's argument, Dostoievski and Kafka are like the negative and positive of the same photograph, each bearing the telltale past and future of the other. The twists and turns of Dostoievski's characters have become, in Kafka, a passive lack of movement in which the universal hero awaits his fate—*our* fate. In the vast distances of Kafka, we can truly measure the intimacies of Dostoievski, and vice versa. The separation of one person from another by so much as a desperate millimeter in Dostoievski becomes, in Kafka, the vast and howling spaces of the immeasurable. In her description and analysis of the relationship between the two writers, Mme. Sarraute achieves the most telling and splendid passages in her book.

Sensitive in the extreme in discussing Dostoievski and Kafka, how can Mme. Sarraute go so wrong in general? Wanting to leave representation—character and action—to the drama and the movies, where recognizable "types" and "situations" are endemic, and to reserve for the novel its singular ability to explore "tenuous states" that lie below the levels of consciousness, Mme. Sarraute seems to be unaware of several important truths.

The meaning of the word *fiction* is "lie," and fiction's enormous power derives from the telling of a lie in which the truth is embodied. A story—the word comes from "history"—exerts a fascination, from the nursery on, because no matter how fantastic the invention, it must contain human truths in order to be either recognizable or meaningful. It is just this tension between invention and reality, between the fictive and the factual that gives the novel its force.

The novel, by its very nature, cannot shun representation in the way, say, that painting can. Whether, as in Mme. Sarraute's novels, where unnamed "characters" reduced to states of being impinge upon a central consciousness, or in "realistic" novels, where people have names like Emma Bovary or Odette de Crécy—and Mme. Sarraute forces us to pretend that Proust was a "realist"—it is impossible for the reader, despite Mme. Sarraute's wishes, not to construe "character" and "story" in the words he reads. Perhaps he is merely lazy and preconditioned; perhaps he wants his attention held; perhaps he doesn't wish each novel to be a harrowing test of his abilities. In any case, the trouble stems from the fact that the reader is already a character in his own mind. And he leads not only an interior psychological life, but one in which, willy-nilly, he is part of a history or a story. It is, again, in the tension that exists between surface reality and inner states that interest lies.

Isn't Mme. Sarraute, therefore, advocating a fiction that removes the very interest and fascination of fiction itself? I think she is. Pure subconsciousness is as boring as pure consciousness. They are only arresting in relation to each other, and are no more detachable than an undertow is from a wave.

Mme. Sarraute, seeing the absurdity of certain conventions of the novel, fails to see that the novel itself is a convention. If one reads Mme. Sarraute's novel *The Planetarium,* for instance, one discovers that in ridding herself of a novelistic trick such as "he said" and "she said," she is forced to be technically obsessive in other directions. Nothing is supposed to get in the way of the "movements" that flow beneath the surface. But what are we to do with the three dots that relentlessly infest every page and interrupt every few phases of Mme. Sarraute's "action"? One becomes suspicious of punctuation. And since there is a realism of the interior that is just as pat as a realistic exterior, one becomes suspicious, finally, of writing itself.

By harping on method, Mme. Sarraute puts herself in the same boat as those critics far more naïve than she who think that counterpoint has been used up because Bach got to the bottom of it, or that iambic pentameter is the falsest tool in poetry because so many bad poems have been written in it, or that representational painting is dead. None of these things is true because they are all technical means to an end. It is splendid that Mme. Sarraute hates the false, the facile, the merely contrived, the old hat. But she should be taken to task for confounding one of the most appalling confusions in aesthetics. New forms do not guarantee new art. Revolutions in art are always revolutions of sensibility, not necessarily of form, though both may occur at the same time, as in the Impressionists. Baudelaire was a great poet not because he wrote sonnets or in spite of the fact that he wrote them. One must have something new to say before one says it; and, if it is new enough, the newness of how it is said will follow. It always has.

Mme. Sarraute is suspicious of convention. We are suspicious of theory. In art, nothing counts but individual talent. Mme. Sarraute's essays prove once again the limitation of theoretical criticism; it is never in a position to create works of genius.

[1963]

Edward Lear
An Introduction

Innocence and humor are by nature fragile, and nonsense, an eccentric species of both, warns us off by definition. Yet at least one thing should be said about it: nonsense is not *non* sense. The senseless is merely irrational, but nonsense holds the plausible and the implausible in tension and makes of the absurd an entertainment, a release, and a form of criticism.

The fine line that separates the rational from the ridiculous is the lifeline of nonsense—a line difficult to draw but all too easy to cross. Nonsense inverts sense without betraying it and requires of its practitioners two qualities rarely found in combination: the ability to think and feel like a child and a highly developed sense of language. The work produced by these anomalous gifts has something of the nature of a game transformed into a special literature.

Sham and pretension—the butts of satire and caricature—are less conspicuously the targets of nonsense.

Yet nothing deflates pretension as much as a change in viewpoint. Certain remarks by children are quoted for the same reason; they see the world from a different angle, and because all of us at one time were capable of doing the same, we recognize that world even if we only dimly remember it. We have forgotten, for instance, that the words "Pago Pago" struck us as odd, even amusing, when we were studying geography; there they were on the map, as incontrovertible as England. Is it any wonder we are delighted to come across Edward Lear's "Gramboolian Plain," with its suggestion of endless space as mysterious as the Russian Steppes, its hint of gremlins, goblins, and ghouls? It sounds so right, somehow, summing up improbable plains in particular and improbable geography in general. Improbability, like hope, leaves just enough room for the possible to squeeze in.

The man who invented—or discovered, as the case may be—the "Gramboolian Plain" was neither a humorist nor a writer professionally. Edward Lear started out as an illustrator of ornithological books—an English version of Audubon. At fifteen he went to work as a commercial artist; at twenty he published his first book, a brilliantly colored compendium of the rarer parrots in the Regent Park Zoo, *Illustrations of the Family of the Psittacidae* (1832). He liked also to sketch, draw, and paint landscapes. Topographical illustration became his lifework and he traveled indefatigably to remote lands in search of the exotic. Birds and landscapes were his original interests. They led him to such faraway places as Greece, Constantinople, the Ionian Islands, Egypt, Albania, Corfu, Malta,

Corsica, and so on. In time these voyages occupied the better part of a life that started twelve years after the beginning of the nineteenth century and ended exactly twelve years before the end of it. At his death, at the age of seventy-six, Lear was a famous man. But, like Lewis Carroll (who was born twenty years after Lear's birth and died twenty years after Lear's death), he was celebrated for his children's books rather than for the work to which he had devoted his life.

There are other similarities to Carroll: both were bachelors who came from large families, both were brought up in worlds dominated by women, and both clung tenaciously to the pleasures and phantasies of childhood. The two masters of nonsense, products of the Victorian Age, were remarkably different personalities. Carroll, a mathematician, had a mind for puzzles, riddles, chess, and logic. Lear was moved by music and the picturesque. Carroll was a Puritan in spirit; Lear was a social and worldly man, if worldliness does not exclude a naïveté endemic to avuncular bachelors of the nineteenth century. He would not— even if he could—have delivered sermons like the Reverend Dodgson on the evils of the theater. Carroll fell in love with pretty little girls. Lear, who had strong emotional attachments to his friends, fell in love with Greece and the Mediterranean. (At various times in his life he was occupied with what he called his "marriage phantasy." It remained a phantasy.) Carroll, with the exception of a trip to Russia, spent his life in his rooms at Oxford. Lear traveled up the Nile, explored India, and built a villa in Italy. He had a distaste for Germans but, atypically, he loathed dogs; the few that make an appearance in Lear's vast menagerie are invariably unpleasant.

Noise, however, was Lear's bête noire. This included snarling, barking, squalling, snoring, coughing, caterwauling—both feline and concert hall—and, in spite of his admiration for children, the sounds of them, so often indistinguishable from those of a well-conducted cat fight. The notorious orchestrations of Rome were particularly galling: "a vile beastly rottenheaded foolbegotten pernicious priggish screaming, tearing, roaring, perplexing, splitmecrackle crachimecriggle insane ass of a woman is practising howling below-stairs so horribly, that my head is nearly off." Lear's hatred of noise had a talented inverse: he had a fine ear for music—the poems make that abundantly clear—and he was a composer of sorts as well. He set many of Tennyson's poems to music, which he sang at social occasions "in a tiny voice but with intense feeling." Archbishop Tait was so moved at one of these performances that he reportedly cried out, "Sir, you ought to have half the laureateship!"—a remark complimentary to Lear but ambiguous in regard to Tennyson.

Lear's father Jeremiah was a rich and virile stockbroker. At one point he owned twelve carriages; at variously divided points he fathered twenty-one children. Ultimately, he landed in King's Bench Prison, in debt and in disgrace. This dismal and sudden descent from riches to rags took place in 1825, when Lear, the youngest child, was thirteen. It was not the sort of event to leave a sensitive child untouched. Like so many sympathetic geniuses, Lear was nearsighted, nervous, bronchitic, and asthmatic, and he loved the wrong things—poetry, for one. His father, Victorian to the last shilling, must have found him an anomaly. A disciplinarian, the elder Lear thought a pleasant weekend pastime was working a blacksmith's forge. He had one installed at Bowman's Lodge, Highgate, the Lear domain, where he manufactured horseshoes to his heart's content. Iron inside and out, the irony never struck him.

Lear's mother, dividing her energies among so vast a brood, never had the importance for Lear that his eldest sister Ann originally and increasingly held for him. (Something of the nature of Lear's mother may be learned from the fact that she brought the incarcerated Jeremiah a full six-course dinner every day during the four years he spent in jail.) After the catastrophic change in fortune, the family dispersed, some of the girls becoming governesses, a few of the children emigrating. Ann, who had an income of her own of three hundred pounds a year, brought Lear up; in fact, she continued being his substitute mother during her lifetime. She inspired, it seems, the usual guilt and affection certain mothers evoke in sensitive sons. The sister and brother were genuinely attached in spite of their many separations, and Lear conscientiously wrote to Ann from every corner of the world. She died when he was approaching fifty. By her death, he was cut off from the only uncritical family love he had ever known.

Lear was educated at home, a fact he sometimes deplored. More often, he extolled the virtues of a natural education over a formal one. His education was special, in any case, but not unenviable: he had a nodding acquaintance with five or six languages, among them ancient and modern Greek. Neither snobbery nor whim accounted for Lear's lack of formal schooling. An epileptic from the age of seven, the affliction plagued him throughout his life. He would mark each seizure in his journal with a small black cross. The disease must not have been of a crippling nature in view of his travels and the incredible amount of work he managed to produce, but it was a constant source of anxiety and depression. Never mentioned to his intimate friends or in his letters to Ann, but only in his journals, his illness was referred to as "the Terrible Demon."

Lear, who had been a rich child and then a poor adolescent, always found himself in financial trouble. Topographical illustration was hardly a gold mine, and money was not easy to come by. To make matters worse, Lear was generous and gave money away when he could least afford to. The number and variety of his friends, many of whom he classified as "swells," constantly amazed him. Both impecunious and something of a social lion, taken up by the rich because of his charm, talent, and availability, the milieu of country houses and elegant drawing rooms turned out to be mutually profitable; he amused and enchanted his friends and confidants, and they in turn commissioned his drawings and paintings. There was nothing calculated about the process. A need, supported by fondness and convenience, was satisfied on both sides. Most of the people Lear liked came from the upper-class world he knew. Devoted to individuals, he came in the end to be bored with society. What good writer hasn't?

One source of his income was, naturally, his published works: his travel books—*Illustrated Excursions in Italy* (1846), *Journal of a Landscape Painter in Southern Calabria* (1852), and others—the nonsense books, and his ornithological and zoological studies, the parrot book of 1832, and *Tortoises, Terrapins and Turtles* (1872). And some money came in from his drawings and paintings. It became his practice to organize exhibitions of his work in England and abroad. These took place at Lear's residence, wherever he happened to be, rather than at professional galleries, in a room reserved for the purpose, which was open to the public one afternoon or day a week. He grew increasingly irritated with idle ladies who swarmed in to look at his paintings, wasted his time, and never bought anything.

Lear, a kind of wandering draftsman, settled down in watering places like Nice and Corfu. They supplied not only an equable climate for his respiratory ailments but also the subjects for his work and the patrons to buy it. His income was perpetually unsteady. A believer in borrowing and lending, he helped less fortunate friends. More fortunate friends helped him, either through loans, gifts, or commissions. The pattern was more or less set as early as 1832, when Lear came to the attention of the thirteenth Earl of Derby, Edward Stanley, who owned a private menagerie at Knowsley. Impressed by the accuracy of Lear's ornithological sketches, Stanley hired Lear to make drawings of his collection. Lear spent four years at Knowsley on this original assignment, and worked, intermittently, for four Earls of Derby over the span of half a century.

It was for the amusement of the fifteenth Earl in particular, the grandson of Edward Stanley—as well as for numerous Stanley grandchildren, nieces, and nephews—that Lear wrote and illustrated his first nonsense book.

The Book of Nonsense was published in 1846, when Lear was thirty-four, and was an immediate success. It consisted entirely of limericks. In the later books, new categories emerged: nonsense alphabets, vocabularies, poems, botany—all profusely illustrated. These various genres were added to as each succeeding nonsense book made its appearance.

The flora and fauna, including human beings, that come to life in the nonsense books have one foot in natural history and the other—sometimes *three* others —in Lear's inexhaustible imagination. Along with honest-to-God storks and pelicans, there are dongs and pobbles; Willeby-wats and Quangle Wangles exist side by side with real-to-life soles and sprats. In geography, several imaginary places take on the fixed attributes of cartography: the already-mentioned "Gramboolian Plain," the hills of "Chankly Bore"—one can almost swear that it was the scene of a famous military engagement—and the "Torrible Zone," which sounds both hemispheric and metaphysical.

The nonsense botany is a splendid mixture of Latin biological terminology and the commonplace: ordinary household objects, familiar insects, etc. "Bottlephorkia Spoonifolia" and "Bluebottlia Buzztilentia" join the more legitimate natural species. My favorite is "Manypeeplia Upsidownia." In the illustration, eight people

—three of whom look amused, three inscrutable, and two (in black) dead—hang upside-down from the branch of a plant.

The alphabets are more seriously pedagogical; *some-one* obviously used them to learn how to read. They work on a simple principle. The capital letter precedes the text, the fifth line uses the same letter in lower case:

N

N was a net,
Which was thrown in the sea,
To catch fish for dinner
For you and for me.

n!

Nice little Net!

There are slight variations on this arrangement in the various alphabets. Similarly pedagogical are the twenty-six "nonsense rhymes and pictures"—mislabeled, since they do not rhyme—in Lear's third nonsense book. They consist of extraordinarily good illustrations of animals, insects, fish, and birds, with a statement underneath. Example:

> The Comfortable Confidential Cow,
> who sate in her Red Morocco Arm Chair and
> toasted her own Bread at the parlour Fire.

These are, evidently, vocabulary builders, though many a vocabulary builder must have surprised his parents by using words like *dolomphious* and *scroobious*.

The creation of words—of which in our time Joyce is the master—was one of Lear's delights. His letters are filled with made-up words; they are not merely devices invented for the sake of the nonsense books, but a language natural to their author. Ranging through the fields of knowledge, drawing on his personal experience, Lear invents words for the sake of words, and words for sounds, creatures, places, and things. Many of the nonsense words echo the sound and meaning of actual words. Plausibility derives from an interchange between the real and the invented. *Scroobious,* for instance, rings changes on *screw, scrobe, Scrooge, scrub, Rube, studious, dubious, scribe,* and so on. And sometimes a nonsense word simply makes us aware of the nonsensical quality of legitimate words, an awareness dulled by familiarity. A "Duckbilled Platypus," an incontestable product of evolution, when placed, even in the mind, in juxtaposition to "Quangle Wangle," reveals its true colors.

Many of Lear's words, created from sound alone, are phonetic misspellings like *eggszibission.* A typical device is to add the *n* of *an* to the noun that follows it: "a nass," "a neasy passage," "a Ninstitution." The last is an example of how a random device can pay an extra dividend in ironic implication. A Ninstitution, I would assume, is a place characterized by the gathering together of ninnies. There are many institutions that can make as great a claim. Something similar holds true of Lear's phrase "hole harmy," where there is a play of meaning on the words *whole, hole, ole,* and *harm.*

Other words are made up to describe the special quality of an event or an object. When an earthquake destroyed Lear's rooms on Corfu, he said they had been "splifficated," and he talks of a ship he sailed on as a "stereoptic sophisticle steamer." More pointed are those words that are in themselves criticisms of what they describe: *mucilaginous monx,* or *foggopolis* as a designation for London, or *a formillier nod* as a description of a greeting from an army man. Some are pure nonsense, like *omblomphious.*

New words filter into a language. Carroll's "Jabberwocky" is enthroned in *Webster's.* And after World War II, *gismo* and *gremlin* became, if not exactly household words, widely used. The creation of words by an individual not only tells us something about the ways words originate in language but also often parodies their creation. And there are words that simply arise out of a need to define something for which no adequate word yet exists—Lear's *flumpy* to describe a sound, for one. Joyce's *funferal* and Lear's *phits of coffin* make comments in themselves. Lear uses every verbal trick: puns, exaggerated phonetic spellings (*fizzicle* is a fine one), hyperboles, cockneyisms, and even Spoonerisms (*Mary Squeen of Cots*).

A caricature is one view of identity. Lear's self-caricature is both verbal and visual. In his famous poem "Self Portrait of the Laureate of Nonsense," which begins, "How pleasant to know Mr. Lear! / Who has written such volumes of stuff! / Some think him ill-tempered and queer, / But a few think him pleasant enough," Lear describes his nose as "remarkably big," his visage as "hideous," his beard as wiglike, and his body as "spherical." Lear was not enchanted by his own appearance. (T. S. Eliot's parody of the Lear poem goes the original one better: "How unpleasant to meet Mr. Eliot!" etc.) In actuality Lear was tall, had a somewhat egg-shaped head with a high forehead, a large beard, a thick nose, and wore glasses. In the illustrations for the limericks, these physical attributes crop up often—the men are usually round-shaped (or very thin, by contrast); the noses are usually exaggeratedly long, thick, or blunt; there are many beards and hirsute eccentricities; and high foreheads are the rule. In fact, in many of the limericks these features are often the subject of the poem. The very first limerick begins, "There was an Old Man with a beard"; and there are innumerable others, like the "Old Person of Tring, / Who embellished his nose with a ring"; the "Young Lady whose nose, / Was so long that it reached to her toes"; the "globular Person of Hurst"; and the "old man in a barge, / Whose nose was exceedingly large."

Lear's limericks have two built-in monotonies. 1: With few exceptions, the first and last lines end with the same word, so that one of the opportunities for ingenuity is lost. 2: The last line is most often a repetition of the first, embellished with an adjective:

There was an Old Man of the Isles,
Whose face was pervaded with smiles:
He sung high dum diddle, and played on the fiddle,
That amiable Man of the Isles.

Crises in the limericks are often resolved by the appearance of "they," who represent a kind of *deus ex machina*: "they" raise questions, mete out just punishments and rewards, are often arbitrary and cruel, and just as often cure, heal, and save. Whether "they" are authorities, the voice of the mob, or guiding or avenging spirits would be hard to say. "They" exist; and occasionally "they" are the victims rather than the victimizers, as in "There was an Old Man with a poker, / Who painted his face with red ochre; / When they said, 'You're a Guy!' he made no reply, / But knocked them all down with his poker." Usually "they" do the knocking down or the smashing.

The limericks at their best are funny, at their middling engaging, and at their worst automatic and self-imitative. They were not intended to be read straight through—there are two hundred and twelve of them—and are best dipped into at random.

If the limericks sometimes seem repetitive, the drawings that accompany them do not. They can be looked at endlessly, for they are inventive and witty and make ingenious use of the possibilities of black and white, in line, density, and contrast. Their chief characteristic is movement; they are wildly active—the nervous products of a mental choreography in which Lear is as much a dancing master as he is a cartoonist. One can see how they have influenced illustration and the cartoon. They anticipate Thurber in particular (see the rabbits in "There was an Old Person whose habits"), are occasionally Steinbergian, and echoes of them appear in the work of Ben Shahn (see "There was an Old Man of the South") and Leonard Baskin (see the raven in "There was an Old Man of Whitehaven"). People, animals, and birds fly, leap, hang, tilt, jump, run, tiptoe, pivot, kick, fall, lurch, balance, and levitate.

I do not think there is a single limerick illustration in which some creature is not partially off the ground. There is a marked vitality in the limbs, hands, and feet, and a good deal of the point of each text is expressed through the eyes and the mouth.

Food is an obsessive preoccupation in the limericks. The characters in the course of the first nonsense book alone manage to consume or imbibe apples, pears, onions, honey, figs, gooseberry fool, beer, camomile tea, rabbits, fish, buns, butter, broth, soup, oil, stew, cake, brandy, soy, bread, muffins, toast, roots, ale, snails, and gruel. I exempt from the above category the "Old Man of Vienna, / Who lived upon Tincture of Sienna," and the Old Man of Leghorn, who was snapped up by a puppy.

Food finally becomes a category of its own in Lear's "Nonsense Cookery," which includes three funny recipes, attributed to a Professor Bosh, for "Amblongus Pie," "Crumbobblious Cutlets," and "Gosky Patties." For the last, the following ingredients are required: a pig, a post, currants, sugar, peas, chestnuts, a candle, turnips, cream, Cheshire cheese, foolscap paper, black pins, brown waterproof linen, and a large broom handle.

The recipes appear in Lear's second nonsense book, *Nonsense Songs, Stories, Botany, and Alphabets* (1871). The book is more famous for other inclusions. "The Owl and the Pussy-cat," "The Jumblies," and the other songs make their debut. There is a delightful tale—the only one, as far as I know—"The Story of the Four Little Children Who Went Round the

World," but it is the poems that make the greatest claim to our attention. And one makes the greatest claim of all.

"The Owl and the Pussy-cat" is one of those rare works of genius that eludes definition; it is inexplicable in its creation and permanent in its effects. It is the romantic poem refined to the absolute essence of romantic poetry; a whole genre of literature translucently shines through it. It is as pure in its own way as Keats's "La Belle Dame Sans Merci." Without having a rational theme, and just possibly having a subject, it uses, almost *sub rosa,* the essential trappings of romanticism: it is a love poem, a voyage takes place in it, a miraculous event occurs, the sea plays a part, and —most important of all—it approaches the condition of music. There is something funny and sad about it, perhaps the impossibility of its events, more probably the original mating itself. An owl and a pussy-cat are not by nature lovers. But, then, neither were Tristram and Isolde. The owl and the pussy-cat, at least, did not have to resort to a love potion. And there is something slightly disturbing, too, in the wisest of all birds and the canniest of all animals making the trip in the first place. We can't help feeling that these two charming creatures are bucking the odds at every turn. If they don't devour each other, if the boat isn't upset so they drown, if the pig doesn't have the ring or decide to sell it for a shilling . . . the suspense is killing. "The Owl and the Pussy-cat" tells a story within the narrow confines of a three-stanza lyric. The story and the telling are haunting. By the time we read

And hand in hand, on the edge of the sand,
    They danced by the light of the moon,
        The moon,
        The moon,
    They danced by the light of the moon.

we have had, like Virginia Woolf's Lily Briscoe, our vision. The repetition of "the moon" is hypnotic. A lesser writer would have omitted the fourth line. There is an absolute balance of elements in "The Owl and the Pussy-cat" in scene, action, diction, and music. It is, of its kind, perfection.

"The Owl and the Pussy-cat" arouses an emotion difficult to locate. Intensity of feeling had no adequate outlet in Lear. In spite of his gregariousness, his lovableness, he was essentially an isolated man. Work and travel never quite quenched his endless search for a perfect friendship, an ideal relationship that would respond to his openness and warmth. And the "Terrible Demon" of epilepsy frequently left him shattered. Though nonsense was neither, strictly speaking, a barrier nor a weapon, it became an emotional modus vivendi, a language to use when feeling—too strong, embarrassed, or uncertain of its response—strived to circumvent the balder denotations of words. The double-edged incongruity of Lear's world stood him in good stead with children, whom he loved and who loved him back. Wherever he went, he became the palace entertainer of the young. But what is funny to a child can be more than funny to an adult. Lear is in the tradition of a certain kind of clown: Harlequin, Petrouchka, and, for us, Chaplin. Because nonsense was a way in which he often expressed his feelings, the poems are full of floating mines. An undercurrent of emotion, an indefinable presence lurks behind the façade of words. Not always, but sometimes. Poems like "The Owl and the Pussy-cat" and "The Jumblies" have a tonal shimmer not present in the purely humorous poems like "The Akond of Swat." To make crybabies of these poems would be absurd; they were not intended to be, nor are they, great emotional outpourings. They contain, nevertheless, more than meets the eye, and a great deal of what they contain results from what reaches the ear. Like all good poems, they communicate more than they seem to be saying; like music, they take soundings of the interior at variable depths. Behind Lear's songs, Tennyson, transfigured by a change in surface, sings away. It is the unique characteristic of poetry—and nonsense poetry at its best defines that characteristic—to communicate the nonverbal through words. That is why Lear has as much influence on literary style as he does on caricature. His poems shed light in several directions: toward the cartoon strip and the animated cartoon, and, more seriously, toward Joyce, Beerbohm, Beckett, and Ionesco. Joyce is obviously Learian, sometimes so much so that in isolated passages it is difficult to tell the two authors apart. Lear wrote, but either might have written, "a sparry in the pilderpips and a pemmican on the housetops." And nonsense is not unconnected with wit. Lear wrote, but a character in Ronald Firbank *might* have said, "Dinners are natural and proper; but late mixed tea-parties foul and abhorrent." The question of early unmixed tea-parties is left hanging.

Lear was a Victorian. He got closer to the fountainhead of his age than most. During the summer of 1846, he gave Queen Victoria a course of twelve drawing lessons, first at Osborne, then at Buckingham Palace. They seem to have got along fine. In writing, Tennyson was the great master and a friend as well, though Emily Tennyson, the laureate's wife, was closer—in fact, Lear's closest confidante. In painting, the Pre-Raphaelites defined the outer reaches of the avantgarde. Though Lear was a friend of both Holman Hunt and Millais and tried their methods, he was not, by sympathy or talent, a Pre-Raphaelite. Some of Lear's drawings seem very advanced, almost Cézanne-like, like the view of Villefranche. His oils are negligible (I go by hearsay, never having seen one), but his drawings are finer than have been acknowledged. Being the laureate of nonsense has overshadowed his achievements as an artist. Great in one, hardly anyone mentions that he was good in the other. His lifelong ambition, to do a series of two hundred drawings to illustrate Tennyson's poems, was never completed. Difficulties of production and reproduction got in the way. Lear was still working on them at the end.

Lear's nonsense books were written to amuse children. They still do. Adults, looking over the shoulders of the young, may be equally amused and sometimes something more. Lear never forgot his childhood—the mark of all good writers. What a child feels is not often the same as what he can say. What an adult can say is not always the same as what he feels. Lear came to the rescue.

[1964]

Denis Devlin
Christic
in the Machine

Though Denis Devlin was an Irishman, he was born in Scotland, and educated in Germany and France. As a member of the Irish diplomatic corps, he was assigned at various times to Italy, the United States, and Turkey. Reared in a parochial setting, he was anything but narrow; yet, as a diplomat, he intensified a process psychologically peculiar to the traveler, the expatriate, and the exile: the farther he traveled from his country the more he represented her. (A line in "The Tomb of Michael Collins" goes: "We love the more the further from we're born!") The loss of innocence is universally historical; in the expatriate and the exile, it can become geographical, and in the diplomat ironic: though the distance between the country of his birth and the world in general is not irreversible, he can only represent his country by leaving her. At the same time, he becomes the very symbol of what he left behind. In Devlin's work, the loss of innocence is complicated by an ambivalent attitude toward Catholicism, magical and exotic on the one hand, dogmatic and local on the other. It would seem that, for Devlin, Catholicism came to stand for a lost locale and a lost innocence as well.

In Ireland, where Catholicism is in the air, faith and the loss of it—or worse, the intellectual renunciation of a religious emotional commitment—are peculiarly complex. National loyalty is involved as well as an obsession with the meaning of betrayal. Catholicism and nationalism, dogma and rebellion are uncomfortable bedfellows. Taken in pairs, they blur the ends of action, a theme of special interest to Devlin. More than most people, Devlin, an official, was in a position of having to act in a state of doubt. Nevertheless, there was something appropriate in his becoming a diplomat; he had studied for the priesthood (an elite) and had fallen in love with foreign languages (which opened choices). He remained loyal to his world by embracing a larger one and stayed national through a process of internationalization, a temperamental tendency from the beginning. A doubly committed man, as aware of the natural nobility of living things as he was of the façades that screened them off, his work rises directly out of his conflicts and is seldom merely rhetorical play-acting. His poems try to rescue every scrap of human feeling from the forces that would destroy them, and the poems name the feelings and their enemies, whether they exist within himself ("The basi-

lisk, my mercy in his eyes, / Unmans us both . . .")
or are as politically definable as "all the world's police /
Round the world's love-bed."

In their introduction to this selected volume, Allen
Tate and Robert Penn Warren make tentative claims
of greatness for three poems: "Lough Derg," "From
Government Buildings," and "The Passion of Christ."
Since their statement of the theme of "Lough Derg"
is concise, I will take the liberty of quoting it: "a
civilized Irishman of the Catholic faith meditates on
the difference between the scepticism of faith and the
simple, fanatical faith of the Irish peasant—with whom
he partly identifies himself—praying at Lough Derg."
(Lough Derg is a Catholic place of pilgrimage in Ireland comparable to Lourdes in France.)

A poem with a major theme, "Lough Derg" falls
short of being a major poem. Why? Lacking the clear
cumulative dramatic line of a poem such as "Sunday
Morning," to which Tate and Warren compare it, its
intelligence is crabbed, squeezing its ideas too tightly
into the armor of its form. Moreover, the metaphorical
unity of "Sunday Morning" is lacking. Stevens, confining his images to birds and fruits, announces them
in his first stanza and weaves them like connecting
threads through each succeeding one. This seemingly
simple-minded structural device is partially responsible
for the clarity of thought, the authority of tone, and
the unity of "Sunday Morning." Stevens's images gradually expand and lead, progressively, to the final sounding of his last line. Devlin bottles up complex notions
and feelings in a rhetoric equally complex, while setting himself technical problems of enormous difficulty.

The technical necessities of the poem obscure the formal ones. "Lough Derg" *seems* controlled by its rhyme, meter, and so on, but a prevailing uniformity of tone and image is missing. At times it is inflated; at times it mistakes tightness for tautness so that, the strain of labor still being visible, the impact of emotion is blunted. In spite of magnificent stanzas, "Lough Derg" is often too exclamatory in the manner of Hart Crane at his weakest, or constricted, as in the couplet ending stanza four: "Clan Jensen! less what magnanimity leavens / Man's wept-out, fitful, magniloquent heavens."

What plagues Devlin as a poet in "Lough Derg" unfortunately mars a great deal of his work; simply put, it is an inability to define the subtle insights of his intelligence, an intelligence at war with, or confined by the very forms through which it is comprehended. Devlin's poems are not only vehicles of emotions and thoughts but attempts to straighten them out. As such, they have the virtue of genuineness and the drawback, often, of inscrutability. More is being said than gets down on paper, and there is sometimes a hollow ring to the conclusion of a poem, as if a summing up were to follow an argument one didn't quite hear. Clogged by too many images competing for attention, by too much happening at once, the poems are like charged high-tension wires firmly connected to one pole but not quite reaching the other. Intensity is never lacking. Point often seems to be.

"The Passion of Christ" retells the story of Christianity in twenty-two short sections. Each section has a separate title such as "The Fall," "The Nativity,"

"Veronica's Veil," and so on. Here is a typical four-line section:

THE MAN OF SORROWS
He sought our sorrow out and bought it back
From merchants in the back streets of the heart:
But we, suspended between love and lack,
　　Will neither sign off nor take part.

It is a simple, clear, fit style for a series of short lyrical poems exploring the implications of a narrative. But one section rises above all the others and typifies Devlin at his best, a combination of verbal fluency—particularly in stanza one—and intellectual penetration—as in the last line:

ASCENSION
It happens through the blond window, the trees
With diverse leaves divide the light, light birds;
Aengus, the God of Love, my shoulders brushed
With birds, you could say lark or thrush or thieves

And not be right yet—or ever right—
For it was God's Son foreign to our moor:
When I looked out the window, all was white,
And what's beloved in the heart was sure,

With such a certainty ascended He,
The Son of Man who deigned Himself to be:
Then when we lifted out of sleep, there was
Life with its dark, and love above the laws.

"From Government Buildings" reaches depths Devlin was to sound at a more profound level in "Memoirs of a Turcoman Diplomat." The protagonist is a dip-

lomat in both poems and the connection between them
is made explicit in the similarity of their first lines.
"From Government Buildings" begins "Evening
lapses. No pity or pain, the badgered . . ." The first
line of "Memoirs of a Turcoman Diplomat" is "Eve-
nings ever more willing lapse into my world's evening."
"From Government Buildings" is a love poem that
sets the psychic realities of the lovers against the
world's boredom and dangers, has religious overtones,
and uncovers an ultimate world of myth and terror
where "When the culture-heroes explored the nether
world / It was voiceless beasts on the move made Death
terrible." Lines like "You, you I cherish with my
learned heart / As in a bombed cathedral town, doubly / A tourist trophy now . . ." exhibit Devlin's kind
of compression, in which a large idea, turned on an
image, is forced into a small compass, where it ex-
plodes its meaning almost as the reader is about to
pass it by. But "From Government Buildings" has typical Devlin difficulties of syntax and punctuation. I
have struggled over the following—the fifth stanza—
without any certainty of understanding Devlin's intention:

Friendship I will not, barring you; to have witness does:
Doll birds, dogs with their social nose, by day
Are touchstone. But at night my totem silence
With face of wood refuses to testify.

Does Devlin mean that to have witness *does* bar
you? If so, why the colon? Or does the phrase of the
second half of line one refer to what follows, as the
punctuation implies? If so, to have witness does what?

There are implications in the words *witness* and *totem* that suggest wider perimeters that come to rest, possibly, in the lines "So is my care though none your mystic I, / Nor you like the painted saints but breath and more" and in the last lines of the poem: ". . . and I would have you / Fingering the ring with its silver bat, the foreign / And credible Chinese symbol of happiness." As a whole, the poem strikes me as moving and permanently interesting, but tantalizing in the possibilities of its interpretation.

There are throughout Devlin's work similar problems of syntax and punctuation that sometimes seem intentional and sometimes barriers to understanding that simple editing would remove. If Devlin presents difficulties, three things should be said in fairness to him: he wrote many lyrics that are as clear as crystal; there is a conscious insistence on the potency of the image rather than on logical syntax; large ambiguities are at the heart of what he deals with. The questions Devlin raises are subtle and his material has an intellectual range not usually found in contemporary poetry, where intelligence often works itself out in merely technical solutions or is abjured altogether. In "Encounter," three worlds are posed against each other: the literary Protestantism of England, the mystical Catholic tradition of Ireland, and the sensuous human culture of France—all in a twenty-line poem. "Jansenist Journey" posits moral good against religious rapture. In "Argument with Justice," two major questions are raised: If justice became a reality, would the vision of heaven disappear? If so, is injustice necessary for religious vision? In "The Blind Leading the Blind," a journey takes place in which the acceptance of danger becomes a possible triumph over it. In "Mother Superior in the City of Mexico," the barbarism of civilized Spain is contrasted with the barbarism of the Aztec Indians. Mexico, a special Catholic culture, is seen caught between "the vulpine Atlantic and the wolf Pacific jaws." Devlin is a poet of ideas, of large oppositions, of more than personal vision.

As a whole, the poems struggle to get back to natural feeling in a world geared to conspire against it, a theme larger than religious skepticism, which is but one battleground in a wider conflict. The question of what natural feeling is rises most crucially in men who have achieved mastery of one kind or another. Having taken some measure of the world, they do not need to achieve what is already theirs and are free to raise questions not only about the nature of the world but about power itself. Authority is a kind of clearheadedness; it strips the world of one of its most persistent dreams while revealing others. It is no accident that Devlin's most probing poems should be centered on heroes— secular or sacred, tragic or ironic—who achieve, relinquish, or disdain power: "The Tomb of Michael Collins," "The Passion of Christ," "From Government Buildings," "Memo from a Millionaire," "Memoirs of a Turcoman Diplomat," "Meditation at Avila," "A Dream of Orpheus," etc. Power is a test of the genuine, not because it is admirable in itself but because it removes that blind spot from vision that the world considers admirable.

The truth and falsity of love is one scale upon which

Devlin weighed the genuine. His use of dreams makes
it clear that, for him, the unconscious was the pro-
foundest touchstone of natural feeling. Though the
diplomacy of the world may work for or against human issues that underlie it, human behavior itself is
a kind of diplomatic conspiracy agreed upon by society
at the expense of feeling. Devlin is constantly aware
of man as an animal trapped in clothing, of the soul as
a reality hovering between the magical and the real.
He is a peculiar kind of mythic poet, contradictory in
the extreme. His worldliness is a measure of the primitive; the "surrealist" nature of much of his imagery is
a focus for what the rational knows to be true. He is,
in short, a man of classical temper putting a wild and
romantic universe in order.

His vision is double, and a characteristic device of
Devlin's is to compress a metaphor into an adjective-
and-noun or a short phrase in which either two forms
superficially incongruous in nature are placed together
—"peasant tiger," "negro mountain," "brute divinities,"
"seaweed crowd"—or to fuse the natural and the in-
animate into a single image: "metal moon," "lightning
like a fever chart," "bandit landmark," "a breastful of
warships," "spider-camera," "knees flashing like scis-
sors," and "the matador swords of the sun." Devlin's
landscape becomes increasingly animated, and because
of the paradoxical nature of his theme, mechanistic.
The polar limits of these images might be set by two
references to Christ: "Christ the Centaur" in "Lough
Derg"; and "The Tears of Christ in the machine," in
"The Passion of Christ."

[1964]

Katherine Anne Porter
Reversing the Binoculars

Praised so often as a "craftsman," a "stylist," and a "master of prose," Katherine Anne Porter must occasionally long to be admired for what she is— a writer. Through an inability to compromise and sheer endurance, Miss Porter, who is an artist, has come to represent Art, and though the role has never obscured the quality of her work, it has shifted attention away from the content of the work itself. The first concern of these stories is not aesthetic. Extraordinarily well-formed, often brilliantly written, they are firmly grounded in life, and the accuracy and precision of their surfaces, so disarmingly easy to read, hold in tension the confused human tangles below. Experience is the reason for their having been written, yet experience does not exist in them for its own sake; it has been formulated, but not simplified.

These stories turn on crises as stories should, but two special gifts are evident: depth of characterization, which is more usually the province of the novelist, and a style that encompasses the symbolic without sacrificing naturalness. Miss Porter is a "realist," but one who knows the connotations as well as the meaning of words. Understatement and inflation are foreign to her; she is never flat and she is never fancy. In the best of her work, the factual and the lyrical are kept in perfect balance. She values the symbol, but she is not, strictly speaking, a symbolic writer. Observed life is the generating factor, and though it may connect with a larger metaphor, it is rooted in the everyday realities of people, situations, and places. The names of the three books collected here supply us with a clue to their author's method: though the stories from which they are drawn have, of course, their singular characters and actions, the title of each suggests a wider meaning. Betrayal in "Flowering Judas," death in "Pale Horse, Pale Rider," and precarious balance in "The Leaning Tower" are both specific and general. Their titles do not belie their particular natures; yet, being themselves, they are more than themselves. They have subjects, but they also have themes.

The clarity of the prose in which these stories are written allows for subtle undercurrents. The qualities of poems—compression, spontaneity, the ability to make connections, and the exploitation of the resources of language—are present, but nothing could be more inimical to Miss Porter's way of doing things than the self-consciousness of "poetic prose." Incident and character are her means; syntax is her instrument; and revelation is her goal. Cocteau once made a distinction between poetry *in* the theater and the poetry *of* the theater. Miss Porter is a poet *of* the short story and she never confuses the issue.

Because the ambiguity of good and evil is the major theme, betrayal is a frequent subject of these stories—betrayal of the self as well as of others. Certain preoccupations reoccur: the hollowness of faith, both religious and political; the mask of charitableness used by the uncommitted and the unloving to disguise their lack of involvement; the eroding effects of dependency; the power of delusion. Many of the characters have something in common: their actions being hopelessly at war with their motives, with the best of intentions, they are lured toward an ironic terror.

Representatives of one of Miss Porter's major notions —since we cannot leave each other alone, it is not always as easy as it looks to tell the victim from the victimizer—they struggle to escape the necessity of confronting themselves, and vaguely hoping to do the right thing, they are hurled into the maelstrom of conflict by forces as mercurial and cunning as those used by the Greek gods. Fate is not, however, an abstraction in these stories; it is more the consequence of character —of weakness, dependence, or the inability to let go of illusion—than it is the drawing out of cosmic plots. Only in "Pale Horse, Pale Rider" do forces outside the self, war and disease, become irrational adversaries.

Evil, to Miss Porter, is a form of moral hypocrisy. In the person of Homer T. Hatch, the malevolent, Lucifer-like catalyst of "Noon Wine," who roams the country collecting rewards on escaped prisoners and mental patients, it operates under the banner of social justice in the cause of profiteering. In Braggioni, the successful revolutionary of "Flowering Judas," it is seen as the degraded daydream of the ideal, which has not only been corrupted by power and sentimentality, but has transformed itself into a complacent form of intimidation. In the two Liberty Bond salesmen who menace Miranda in "Pale Horse, Pale Rider," it takes on the totalitarian cloak of enforced "patriotism."

Moral hypocrisy can disguise itself as anything from a worldwide political movement to self-delusion. But the self-deluded are not necessarily evil. In fact, they can evoke our sympathy—perhaps treacherously—but are distinguished from the evildoer by two important facts: evil is single-minded—a rough definition of it in the canon of Miss Porter's fiction might simply be that view of life that cannot see that everything is at least two-sided—and it lies in a special way by producing terror in the *name* of good. By having the power—or worse, by being given it—to impose its vision of the world on other people, it destroys.

The nature of how and why power is given, where the distinction between the victim and the victimizer gets blurred, is the subject of "Theft." More than a purse is stolen; identity and self-respect are lost by a middle-aged woman who allows herself to be victimized. The innocent can be made to feel guilty. But Miss Porter brings up an unpleasant question: By *allowing* themselves to be *made* to feel guilty, are they *not* guilty? The problem becomes more profound as the field widens or deepens. In "The Leaning Tower," the identity and self-respect of a whole nation is at stake.

In "Noon Wine," the very nature of what guilt, identity, and self-respect really are is brought under scrutiny.

Miss Porter can reverse the binoculars either way; she is after the small despot as well as the large one. No one knows better than she that tyranny begins at home. The egotism, pride, and self-pity of the Germans in "The Leaning Tower" have their domestic counterparts in an American family in "The Downward Path to Wisdom." It ends with a little boy singing a song to himself that goes "I hate Papa, I hate Mama, I hate Uncle David, I hate Old Janet, I hate Marjory, I hate Papa, I hate Mama . . ." The little boy, unlike some of the characters in "The Leaning Tower," has not yet learned to hate whole races and nations, but since his song is an early composition, the chances that he will are good.

The closest thing to a spokesman the author allows herself is called "Miranda," but the one truly innocent world that emerges from these stories can be found in the eight reminiscences of the South that were originally published in "The Leaning Tower." Officially "fiction," they seem to be creations of pure memory and are filled with the sights and sounds of childhood recollection. Beyond this limited nostalgia, innocent but often painful, only the natural and the primitive remain undamaged by the counterclaims of the world.

That may be why Miss Porter's two favorite settings are Texas and Mexico. In both, a primitive view of life does not exclude what is morally decent and necessary. The Indian peasants in the Mexican stories, the farmers and Negroes in the Southern ones are neither good nor bad in any conventionally moral sense. They may be violent, but they act from an implicit set of values in which instinct and feeling have not yet been corroded. The heroine of "Maria Concepcion" kills her rival but is protected from the police by her friends—and even her enemies—in a pact as ancient as jealousy and murder. Morality is pragmatic and involves the living; the mere fact of being alive is more important than justice for the dead.

A different but analogous situation confronts Miranda in "Old Mortality." Nurtured on a romantic version; having come to doubt her life, at least, she will separate truth from falsehood—"in her own mind, for herself," Miss Porter adds. But the tered on the continuation of life; it is less concerned with truth as a specific fact, and least of all with truth as an abstract generalization. Maria Concepcion is separated from Miranda by a wide gulf. Maria has faith in life, whereas Miranda puts her trust in the truth. Over and over in these stories, they turn out not to be the same thing. Maria (like Mr. Thompson in "Noon Wine") commits an act of murder that is, paradoxically, an act of faith in life. Miranda (like Laura in "Flowering Judas" and Charles in "The Leaning Tower") has no faith in the name of which an act can be committed.

Miss Porter has added to this collection of her three books of stories a magnificent new long one, "Holiday," three shorter ones, and a modest preface. Good as most of these stories are, they are overshadowed by one work.

If it is the function of the artist to produce a master-piece, Miss Porter may rest easy. In "Noon Wine" she has written a short novel whose largeness of theme, tragic inevitability, and steadiness of focus put it into that small category of superb short fiction that includes Joyce, Mann, Chekhov, James, and Conrad. A study of the effects of evil, it is a story one can turn around in the palm of one's hand forever, for so many meanings radiate from it that each reading gives it a new shade and a further dimension. Without once raising its voice, it asks questions that have alarmed the ages, including our own: When a good man kills an evil man does he become evil himself? If the answer is yes, then how are we to protect ourselves against evil? If the answer is no, then how are we to define what evil is? It is one of the nicer ambiguities of "Noon Wine" that the two "good" men in it commit murder while the one character who is "evil" does not.

In the fateful meeting of the farmer, Mr. Thompson, the deranged Swedish harmonica player, Mr. Helton, and the devil's salesman, Mr. Hatch, Miss Porter has constructed one of those dramas that seem not so much to have been written as discovered intact, like a form in nature. In the perfection of "Noon Wine," Miss Porter has achieved what she has worked for—the artist in total command, totally invisible.

[1965]

Elizabeth Bishop
All Praise

Since the nineteenth century, three versions of the poet as dreamer have become discernible: a person idyllically free of social obligations who takes notes on the beauties of nature; a visionary describing a mythological universe of the past or a Utopian one of the future; and an explorer of the unconscious. This triple notion has advantages: it allows the naturalist to be an innocent in a world of corruption; the mythologist or Utopian to criticize the world by analogy or overtly; and the psychologist to mine the corruption within himself. It has its dangers, too: the note-taker can degenerate into the dilettante; the visionary into the crackpot; and the explorer of the dark into the dark itself—it is only half a step from the dream to the nightmare. What has resulted are three sometimes overlapping traditions: descriptive poetry; poetry of nostalgia or social disaffection (in which either the past or the future becomes preferable to the present); and poetry of personal alienation.

In *Questions of Travel,* Elizabeth Bishop's first book of poems since 1955, we do not find the nostalgic phantasist, the prophetic seer, or the social critic—except by implication. And we aren't being let in on the secrets of her diary, either. We would seem to be dealing with a descriptive poet. It is part of the originality of these poems to elude that category, and, in fact, all others. Though these poems take stock of the beauties of nature, as well as its ugliness, with unique exactitude, that is not their major point or merit. Miss Bishop's precision of image is well known and rightly praised. But it is her viewpoint that is wholly exceptional. Observation and temperament have become inseparable; telling the truth is a form of human sympathy, not a moral imperative or scientific curiosity. Since truth is variable and always suspect, how do we know we're being told it? The credibility of these poems derives from a shocking fact: Miss Bishop is completely sane.

The power of these poems is a result of their clarity. By seeing so clearly, their author achieves effects more exciting often than those the unconscious can drag up by way of association and connection. And we, who have become so used to equating calmness with dullness, are surprised to find in her work a further stretch of the imagination. These poems are far from simple, but they can be easily read; all the preparatory work has been done underground. By not using rose-colored or dark glasses, Miss Bishop has retrieved certain Edens and hells that have been obscured by poets whose vision is distorted or who can hardly see at all. She neither ascends into optimism nor descends into murk. A clearly lighted equanimity allows for every note of the scale, including that intensity from which every blur and distraction have been erased. Disinterestedness has become passionate. She has made sanity interesting without lecturing us about it.

Reading these poems, we have the sensation of seeing what things are *really* like, and we take Miss Bishop's authority for granted. It is an authority that rests on discarded temptations; nothing that has not been isolated to be examined, nothing that has not been delineated sharply has been permitted to be written down. These poems are so pure that sometimes we feel their author has been fed on a secret literature unknown to the rest of the world. Has she read the histories of stones, mountains, and waterfalls in their original languages? If so, she has translated them superbly by passing them through a mind so free to receive them that every object is justly valued, each feeling, each thought allowed its true nature.

If all this suggests that Miss Bishop is naïvely in love with the universe, I hasten to qualify the thought. She is ironic, not sentimental. Anyone who thinks these new poems (and one marvelous story) are love letters to the world or impeccably written picture postcards of Miss Bishop's various stopovers in foreign places would be mistaken. Place is important to her not only because she is a traveler but because the world itself is in exile. She is constantly luring it home by pointing out to it its features. They are not always pretty—an armadillo is not armored against fire, Bedlam is no farther away than St. Elizabeth's in Washington, D.C.—but they are always believably used, not exhibited.

No one could be less precious than Miss Bishop, and

no one could be less sociological. Who else could write
a poem about a "squatter tenant"—"the world's worst
gardener since Cain"—in which the idea of condescension would be merely vulgar? The author doesn't insist
on being human, because she is, and what makes her so
is unselfconsciousness and accuracy. Each demands a
great deal of the other. To lie about the world or to rant
about it is not to cherish it. Miss Bishop is civilized in
a special way: in being herself and in telling the truth,
she supersedes manners by setting superior standards.
By choosing so carefully what and whom she sees, she
is never forced toward the half-lie. What is here in
place of manners is a rare combination of naturalness
and elegance—elegance of mind, spirit, taste—the real
thing, for it is neither learned nor fashionable, but inherent. Not being rarefied there is no need to be colloquial. Miss Bishop never confuses the natural with the
primitive or the elegant with the mannered—their debased counterparts. And what is more to the point, she
couldn't.

She is an instinctive storyteller, too faithful to the
truth to use what passes for the devices of drama. She
has had to create a small theater of her own in which
character and setting become dramatic not through odd-
ity or conflict but through the charm, the suscepti-
bility of the perceiver. It is a theater of depths as well as
surfaces, and it both suggests and defines where questions of travel are truly answered. The last line of "Arrival at Santos" reads, "we are driving into the interior." Only someone unfamiliar with Miss Bishop's
way of doing things would have to be told that what
she means by the interior is more than geographical.

Few poets are so clearly in touch with the whole of themselves, so able to move from what they see to what they feel without a shift in emphasis. In each poem, Miss Bishop travels right to the center of the bull's-eye. But her own eye exists in two worlds, somewhat like the hero of an earlier poem, "The Gentleman of Shallot," who is bisected by the edge of a mirror. The mirror points out a biological truth: the body is bilaterally symmetrical. But that body—half in, half out of the mirror—is comparable to the poet's viewpoint: every reflection is used as a comment on human experience; but each reflection, clearly, is not all there is to say about it. These poems are profoundly modest. Objects reveal the subjects of the poems more tellingly than might at first be apparent—the real horse in "In the Village" is a counterweight nature supplies to the mother's scream, which is unnatural; the fake horse in "Twelfth Morning; Or What You Will" tells us a great deal about Balthazár's song and his life—but it is never called to our attention that Miss Bishop reveals the object. It is simply handed to us, generously, with no fuss.

Though its contents page divides *Questions of Travel* into two sections, it consists, really, of three: eleven poems set in Brazil, a short story—"In the Village"— and eight poems set elsewhere.

In "Brazil, January 1, 1502," Miss Bishop is free to write of nature as a tapestry because she sees the hand that wove the tapestry as well:

> Januaries, Nature greets our eyes
> exactly as she must have greeted theirs:

> every square inch filling in with foliage—
> big leaves, little leaves, and giant leaves,
> blue, blue-green, and olive,
> with occasional lighter veins and edges,
> or a satin underleaf turned over;
> monster ferns
> in silver-gray relief,
> and flowers, too, like giant water lilies
> up in the air—up, rather, in the leaves—
> purple, yellow, two yellows, pink,
> rust red and greenish white;
> solid but airy; fresh as if just finished
> and taken off the frame.

Who else would have thought of "up, rather, in the leaves" or "solid but airy," both of which so exactly underscore the points they are making? And who else could have used the alliterations of "filling, foliage, underleaf, ferns, relief, flowers, fresh, finished, and frame" so naturally in fifteen lines that we scarcely notice them?

If we follow what Miss Bishop does with the sound of the letter *v*, an intuitive architecture becomes apparent. There are no *v*'s in the first line and none in the last four. In between, where the leaves pile up in density—"yellow, two yellows"—we have the *v*'s of "have, every, leaves, leaves, leaves, olive, veins, over, silver, and leaves," echoes of the letter *f*, this second group of repeated sounds making a subtle background music for the first.

The mysteries that lie behind the ordinary are revealed in *Questions of Travel,* but how Miss Bishop

manages to make proportion and reserve emotional is
hard to say. "The Riverman," where the magical can
only be described in terms its native narrator knows,
suggests how she sticks to the facts and transforms
them:

> and the moon was burning bright
> as the gasoline-lamp mantle
> with the flame turned up too high,
> just before it begins to scorch.

In the first two stanzas of "Twelfth Morning; or What
You Will," not an ounce of inflation or a shred of
rhetoric compete with what is being said:

Like a first coat of whitewash when it's wet,
the thin gray mist lets everything show through:
the black boy Balthazár, a fence, a horse,
  a foundered house,

—cement and rafters sticking from a dune.
(The Company passes off these white but shopworn
dunes as lawns.) "Shipwreck," we say; perhaps
  this is a housewreck.

Miss Bishop is one of the true masters of tone. She
has an absolute sense of what the English language can
do, of how much to say, how much to leave unsaid.
There is no fiddling around with syntax, no *evident*
concern with the sounds of words, no special effects of
typography. We never have to search for a verb or
wonder if a pronoun has an antecedent. What she
brings to poetry is a new imagination; because of that,
she is revolutionary, not "experimental." And she is

revolutionary in being the first poet successfully to use all the resources of prose.

Her poems are so natural to read that they seem to teeter on that edge, where, for a moment, we think, "Why all this could be changed into prose—fine prose indeed, but prose still." But if one tries, say, to write out a Bishop poem as if it were prose, one soon realizes it is impossible to do so. These poems do not advertise themselves in any "poetic" way. We are constantly under the impression that Miss Bishop is in the room with us, speaking, but not making a speech. The voice is friendly but not cajoling, warm but not insistent. She doesn't pretend that she never heard a word longer than a monosyllable or try to dazzle us with the reaches of her vocabulary. In her use of English grammar, she avoids both distortion and excess baggage. It would take some careful searching to find the words *which* or *that* in these poems. Each is a concentrated action that develops organically; prettiness or bombast do not dilute the concentration, and overreaching never interferes with the development. It is relevance as well as accuracy that makes Miss Bishop the fine poet she is. Nothing is turned aside that sheds light; nothing is included that is superfluous. We are in the presence of someone using the orchestra of human speech who doesn't reach down for the drums or up for the harp. We are enchanted to have escaped, for once, the banal and the purple. The result is more than a formal and aesthetic triumph; it is a moral one. Miss Bishop teaches us something precisely because she would be the last person in the world who would want to.

And what we learn—and only by example—is that

objectivity need not be impersonal. Miss Bishop has a clear eye, not a clinical one. A poem like "First Death in Nova Scotia," with its careful understatement, fidelity to detail, and meticulous perception remains completely spontaneous. It is in distancing that its author transcends what in lesser writers is merely verisimilitude. She is a master of perspective as well as tone, for we are in the exact center of what would appear to be conflicting forces: painting and drama, austerity of expression and a personal letter. The intervening layer of the writer seems to have evaporated; we are directed to the material as if neither time nor a persona separated the reader from what he is reading.

In "First Death in Nova Scotia," Miss Bishop is describing her small, dead cousin, Arthur, laid out in a coffin "In the cold, cold parlor . . ." On a marble-topped table there is a stuffed loon, shot by Arthur's father, who is also named Arthur. (And what a nicety that turns out to be by the time we have finished the poem.) What Miss Bishop does with this interplay of dead images is remarkable. Though she never says so—she just lets *us* say so—there must have been a strange connection in the child-observer's mind between dead cousin Arthur and the dead loon. Wasn't the loon's death caused by Arthur's chief mourner, his father? *That* fact would have escaped almost anyone but Miss Bishop. But when, in describing the loon, she says:

> He kept his own counsel
> on his white, frozen lake,
> the marble-topped table.
> His breast was deep and white,

> cold and caressable;
> his eyes were red glass,
> much to be desired.

more than a single intention becomes clear in the last line. Miss Bishop doesn't say, "which *I* much desired." Much to be desired by whom, then? By Arthur's father? Of course; he shot the loon. But the loon's eyes were not red glass *then*. By the child observer? Of course; red glass in all that white! By the loon itself? Just possibly, for hasn't he achieved a *kind* of immortality—the kind that will never be Arthur's?

In the unexpected and resounding "much to be desired," Miss Bishop shows us who she is. It is in the difference between desiring red glass and desiring to kill the loon and being capable of doing so that the distance between the child and the adult, the unawareness of death and the knowledge of it, is measured. And in the barely perceptible rhyme of "caressable" and "red glass," we see how delicately, how forcefully she can work.

Here is the last stanza:

> They invited Arthur to be
> the smallest page at court.
> But how could Arthur go,
> clutching his tiny lily,
> with his eyes shut up so tight
> and the roads deep in snow?

The sudden release of the last line in a poem so compressed that each word is utterly necessary has the impact of a memory held under pressure which is suddenly allowed not to explode but to expand endlessly. Arthur's eyes are shut tight; outside, all Nova Scotia lies dead in winter. But it is the word *roads* that has such large reverberations. Roads are where one goes; Arthur not only wasn't going; he never would be. What the child-observer could not see then is clear now. Arthur could not have walked the roads whether his eyes were open or shut or whether the roads were cleared or deep in snow. And it has taken all the time between Arthur's death and the writing of this poem to discover that—or at least to say so. To point out what Miss Bishop does with the word *forever* earlier in the poem would only illustrate further how subtle straightforwardness can be.

"In the Village" is a story in which indirection pins down a world that is tangible, crystal-clear, and, I would think, permanent. Without using any of the conventional trappings of narrative—exposition, transition, climax—a childhood day surrounds the dark core of a mother's illness. A scream hangs over an idyll and each underlines and comments on the other. An audacity of imagination and a temperance of spirit shape it, as they do the poems in *Questions of Travel*. This new book can only add substance to Miss Bishop's reputation. And that is a strange one. Her work has hardly been ignored; she has won just about every distinction and prize a poet can. But her poems are oddly unknown to the public, even that part of it that is supposed to be interested in poetry. And if obscurity is a general issue in the public's ignorance of poetry, it is not an issue here. Admired by critics, poets, and anyone genuinely interested in writing, her work is not easily labeled. Having no thesis, standing for no school of writing or thought, she is not the kind of poet who attracts public attention. This is partly due to a reticence in the writer herself, to the fact that she has lived in Brazil for the last decade, but mostly to the independence and quality of the poems themselves. Miss Bishop is not academic, beat, cooked, raw, formal, informal, metrical, syllabic, or what have you. She is a poet pure and simple who has perfect pitch. These new poems should be welcomed not only because they are so absolutely and obviously first rate, but because they are one of the few examples of lucidity left in the world.

[1966]

Henry James
The
Imperial Theme

In *The Golden Bowl,* James has written a book open to interpretation but without a specific frame of reference. The temptation to supply one has not gone begging; *The Golden Bowl* may turn out, in the end, to have as many diversified readings as the Bible. There is the Swedenborgian view, supported by Quentin Anderson, who sees the book as the last of a triad composing a "divine novel." Caroline Gordon, outlining a Catholic view, believes that "*caritas*—Christian charity" is "James's secret." Stephen Spender views it as a prediction of the smashup of Western civilization; R. P. Blackmur as a parable about ideal (rather than divine) love; and the late F. O. Mathiessen interpreted it as a realistic novel that fails because of a lack of credibility. Francis Fergusson has written two essays on *The Golden Bowl.* In the second, he agrees, more or less, with Quentin Anderson's notions. In an earlier essay (and to a less extent in the later essay), he sees it as an exploration of the imperial theme. He says, "The historic dimension of the novel may be described as the theme of empire, or rule, with its connotations of worry and glory."

I think Mr. Fergusson was, and is right: *The Golden Bowl* is a novel of empire, and James carefully develops two metaphors in relation to his theme: the illusion of space (travel), and the accretion of treasure (gold). The imagery of the novel falls under the domination of either of these tropes.

The imagery is often out of keeping with the action, but is always related to the theme, for instance, exotic images of distance and movement: the pagoda, the caravans, the desert. It would not be completely inaccurate to see the novel as something like St. John Perse's *Anabasis* with a moral and dramatic action placed at the heart of the imagery.

Most critics see *The Golden Bowl* as a novel with four major characters, Maggie, Adam, Charlotte, and the Prince, and a kind of Greek chorus-duo, Fanny and Charles Assingham—the four major characters being the actors, the Assinghams commenting on the action almost exclusively in a series of question-and-answer analyses of the possible meanings of each action. But there is a seventh character, a minor one in the action, but a major one thematically: the shopkeeper who almost sells the bowl to Charlotte and the Prince, then sells it to Maggie, and finally comes to see Maggie to tell her that the bowl is cracked. He speaks Italian (like the Prince) and English (like

Maggie) and he is Jewish, an important link to James's theme. Though he is a dealer in antiques and gold, he comes to see Maggie because of a *moral* scruple. It is only when he sees the picture of Charlotte and the Prince that he tells Maggie of their earlier interest in the bowl. Through his moral act, Maggie discovers two things; proof of the relationship between Charlotte and the Prince, and a means of dealing with that proof by example. The shopkeeper combines two important notions: he is a temporary owner of the very kind of treasure Adam and Maggie are trying to buy up in Europe with which to stock Adam's museum in American City; and he makes the ethical gesture that releases Maggie, and transforms a morally naïve child into a human being faced with moral alternatives.

Thematically, the book may be viewed this way: Adam and Maggie are Protestants. Europe was Catholic before it was Protestant. But a major idea in the novel is that Europe, if one goes back far enough, was Jewish. Behind the Prince there lies the long history of Western civilization. In order to "collect" that history, Maggie and Adam "buy" up their artifacts, of which the Prince is one. The Catholic Prince is merely the end product of a vast tradition of things and feelings that began in Jewish history and developed out of it. The question the novel asks is: To whom does the golden bowl belong? The Jew who sells it? The Catholic it is bought for? Or the Protestant who buys it?

Early in the novel, we are told that the Prince had an illustrious ancestor. Maggie says, "It was the generations behind you, the follies and the crimes, the plunder and waste—the wicked Pope the monster of them all, whom so many volumes in your family library are all about . . . Where, therefore, without your archives, annals, infamies would you have been?"

And in the same chapter, the Prince is thinking of his family, who have come to London for his wedding: ". . . his younger brother, who had married before him, but whose wife of Hebrew race, with a portion that gilded the pill, was not in condition to travel . . ." (How much is contained in those few lines: the explicit mention of travel, the metaphor of gold, and the close connection between the Catholic aristocracy and Jewish wealth.)

Moreover, in describing Fanny Assingham, James says, "Her richness of hue, her generous nose, her eyebrows marked like those of an actress—these things, with an added amplitude of person . . . seemed to present her insistently as a daughter of the south, or still more of the east, a creature formed by hammocks and divans, fed upon sherbets and waited upon by slaves. . . . She was, in fact, however, neither a pampered Jewess nor a lazy Creole; New York had been, recordedly, her birthplace and 'Europe' punctually her discipline. She wore yellow. . . . she put crimson and gold in her tea-gown. . . . the eyes of the American city looked out, somehow, for the opportunity of it, from under the lids of Jerusalem. . . ."

The selling of the golden bowl is echoed in a later scene in the book, in which another Jewish "merchant," Mr. Suessman, sells Adam a priceless memento. This is the second in a series of four scenes in which a line in the theme becomes clear: the scene in the shop

between Charlotte and the Prince, in which the priceless object is seen to be defective and is not bought;
the scene, an inverse of the first, where a priceless
object is authenticated and *is* bought from a second
Jewish "merchant" by Adam in front of Charlotte; the
scene in which the bowl is bought by Maggie, who
does not see its defect; a corollary scene, where the
bowl is brought to Maggie by the shopkeeper who ex-
poses the defect. The bowl then breaks into three pieces.
In terms of the action of James's story, these three
pieces may symbolically represent the triangles the
major characters are caught in: Maggie-Adam-the
Prince; Maggie-Charlotte-the Prince; Maggie-Char-
lotte-Adam; Charlotte-Adam-the Prince. Thematically,
the three fragments of the bowl may be seen as Protestant, Catholic, and Jewish.

It is a symbolic Jerusalem that Mr. Verver is trying to establish in American City—a museum to house
the contents of Europe. And it is both ironic and profound that he is exiled to this new Jerusalem in Protestant America while Maggie is exiled from it in a Catholic Europe whose roots reach back into Jewish history.
Both these moral journeys, each ending up with its
aesthetic triumph, are expensive. For Maggie, the ethical victory costs nothing less than her father and his
America; for Adam, nothing less than his daughter
and her Europe.

A great human error is examined in *The Golden
Bowl*: the conception of civilization as a material object
rather than a moral experience. When Maggie says to
her father, "Now you may understand the measure
of the love that warms me toward you, when I forget

our nothingness and treat shades as solid things," she announces the insight of the novel's action.

To possess the civilization of Europe by material means alone is not possible. Maggie and Adam are forced to experience aesthetic objects as symbols, their fundamental meaning. (The point is underlined in the physical destruction of the bowl itself.) And they must undergo, as well, the ethical suffering of the civilization that produced these objects in order to understand what that meaning is. Through the pain of a sacrificial ordeal, Maggie comes to know the real value of the golden bowl. Physically cracked, morally priceless, she is condemned to pay its true fee, a price all of Adam Verver's American millions cannot meet.

[1966]

Proust, Chekhov,
James, Mann:
Notes on Fiction

In Chekhov's plays and stories, we have a sense of not being led anywhere, of things just happening. Their naturalness and casualness suggest, when they end, that it is time for the storyteller to go to bed. This effect comes from Chekhov's lack of interest in luring us on to a dramatic conclusion and his detestation of moral preaching. In Chekhov's writing, a moral compass points the way; its true north is "No Lying."

Chekhov externalized the interior of his characters without relinquishing the surface aspects of realism. In his plays, people act out their dreams, yet what they say and do, from moment to moment, seems perfectly ordinary. The monologue was oddly useful in this respect: the governess's speech that opens the second act of *The Cherry Orchard,* or Astrov's long dissertation on trees in *Uncle Vanya*. Chekhov is able to treat psychological nuances as material facts, to make it seem just as real for a character to say, "I am in mourning for my life," as it is for another to say, "They'll be starting the show soon." Chekhov's characters emit words like bird cries, as if they were spontaneously forced out of themselves by internal pressure.

Chekhov has a quality to be found equally in good journalism and good fiction, and for opposite reasons. In the first, the quality of tone never sabotages the verity of fact. In the second, the verity of fact never menaces the quality of tone. A journalist doesn't need a theme since he already has a subject. A fiction writer has a theme and is looking for a subject. (Reason why detective stories can never become literature: no matter how ingeniously devised, how brilliantly written, they are not thematic. They depend on two things, suspense and local color. A good detective story presents the reader with an exotic world; the unknown is made credible. The accuracy of details, or their seeming accuracy, is of tremendous importance, more so than in an ordinary novel because the nature of the fiction— the story—is less plausible. Place and geography are major sources of fascination. But the world is getting smaller. The final detective story will be set in a suburb in Iceland.)

There's a certain point in every novel where one wants to know what everyone had for dinner. Tolstoy is very good on this score, James very bad. There are no bathrooms or kitchens in *The Wings of the Dove* or *The Golden Bowl* (though there is a famous omelette in *The Ambassadors*). Proust offers us a kitchen, a latrine, and a brothel.

Realism supplies us with the number of manhole covers on a particular street. Naturalism splashes around in the sewer.

Chekhov's great victory: the greatest style is to have none. The impenetrable barrier of perfection. Not that he is a greater writer than Tolstoy or Proust. He is more critically inaccessible by seeming so *simple*. Advocates of the New Criticism would go mad if they had nothing to work on but Chekhov. Unlike Joyce, Kafka, and Proust, after a certain point, quickly reached, there is practically nothing to say.

Chekhov: Suicide or murder by gun. Vanya tries to kill the Professor in *Uncle Vanya* and fires two shots, and misses. Treplev shoots himself at the end of *The Sea Gull*. Ivanov shoots himself at the end of *Ivanov*. At Babkino, in 1885, before he had ever seriously thought of himself as a playwright, Chekhov dressed up as a Bedouin and acted out a mock play with Levitan, the painter. Chekhov shot blank cartridges at Levitan from behind the bushes.

The peculiar correspondences in the lives of Chekhov and Keats. Both studied to be doctors; suffered from tuberculosis; died young—Keats at 26, Chekhov at 44 —and in a foreign country. Chekhov died in Germany, Keats in Italy. Keats feared he could not write an epic poem. Chekhov feared he could not write a novel.

In James, homosexuality is a secret theme. *The Sacred Fount* is the most puzzling of his novels, I think, because James got closest to the subject and, because of a lack of adequate transformation, found himself creating more and more mystification to throw the reader —or perhaps himself?—off the scent. It is a novel about the artist, finally, but if he could have been more explicit, as Mann was in *Death in Venice,* he could have had his symbolic "reverberation" twice over. Voyeurism is essential to both James and Proust but not to Mann. James, attempting to deal with it by implication in *The Sacred Fount,* obscures what he's after. Proust succeeds because the scenes that involve homosexuality and voyeurism are explicit and direct: at Montjouvain, in the Duchesse's courtyard, in the peephole scene in the male brothel.

The voyeur is connected with the writer for an obvious reason: The problem of viewpoint. At what point does the observer close in on the peeping Tom? Proust and James deal with viewpoint as an essential part of the work itself. There is no reality without a viewer. How far should one go in including him? Proust went as far as it is possible to go.

The parody as an unconscious compliment: To have read someone closely enough to produce an acceptable imitation, to have become obsessed to the necessary degree requires an attention and concentration the works of most authors never receive. Beerbohm's *The Mote in the Middle Distance,* which James might have considered cruel, says more about James's style than most critics.

If one were to think of a movie about the invention of the camera photographed by the very camera that was being invented one would have the clue to the technical device Proust employs in *Remembrance of Things Past*.

Metaphor is the key to an understanding of Proust. *Remembrance of Things Past* is a book conceived as a poem and written as a novel, a far different thing from a novel written in "poetic prose." The poetry lies in the conception as well as the execution. Feeling and thought are so finely molded to metaphor that the sensibility by which things are apprehended is indistinguishable from the intelligence that later analyzes the nature of sensibility itself. Proust is a great writer and a great thinker; the fact that no serious division can be made between them is an enormous triumph.

We get to know the canvas of *Remembrance of Things Past* in the same way we get to know our own lives. We do not remember consecutively and we do not remember at will. It is these two strange and over-riding facts of human memory that Proust exploits. It is re-experience rather than experience that is valuable. Experience occurs in time but re-experience *may* occur outside it.

We know every sensation, thought, and connection of Marcel's life more thoroughly than we do the people we think we know best in our own lives. One of the secrets of art is that it takes over the function we mistakenly assume belongs to love. Do we ever truly enter into the personality of another being? In Proust, love sets up a barrier of necessity and compulsion that art is free of.

There are two major original ideas in *Remembrance of Things Past:* the true nature of reality exists within ourselves, not outside us; the clue to human salvation lies in the past, not the future.

Chekhov said, "If in the first act you hang a pistol on the wall, then in the last act it must be shot off." Proust might have said, "If in the first act you hang a pistol on the wall, and in the last act it is shot off, then you must build the wall."

Chekhov: "to reveal [people] as they really exist and not as they appear in real life . . ." Very close to Proust, except that after Proust got through with appearances, the matter of existences became questionable.

Chekhov's wit (from a letter): "Now I have four places to live, and I ought to have a wife in each, so that after my death all of them could assemble on the shore of Yalta and tear each other's hair out."

Proust's wit: ". . . there are almost as many deaths as there are people. . . ."

Both Chekhov and Proust had a firm grip on reality and both were absolutely truthful. Proust analyzes and concludes. Chekhov presents and reveals.

"The Black Monk" is not characteristic of Chekhov's other stories, but of Chekhov as a writer. A certain withheld mysticism one senses behind many of the other stories is allowed to occupy the foreground.

I can see no reading of "The Black Monk" other than as a fable of the artist. As such, it is similar in theme to Mann's *Death in Venice* and James's *The Aspern Papers*. The experience of the narrator in the first two stories is extreme—in Chekhov, madness; in Mann, disease; but in the James, where the narrator does not represent the artist, it is reduced to a petty crime, thievery. The point in James is that the narrator is trying to get the experience secondhand, trying to get the papers without experiencing what made them possible. He wants to possess the secrets of art without paying for them morally. That is why he fails; he must relinquish the papers or marry Tina in order to get them, must go through some version of the original relationship between Aspern and Juliana that led to the creation of the poems. (This idea is later elaborated in *The Golden Bowl,* where, to possess the artifacts of a civilization, the characters are forced to experience the moral crises of civilization.) What are fables of the artist in Chekhov, Mann, and James become myth in Proust. Marcel is his Aschenbach, Swann the anonymous narrator of *The Aspern Papers,* and Charlus his Black Monk.

Chekhov disliked Ibsen's plays and admired Maeterlinck's. Peculiarly understandable even if an error in judgment. Chekhov was closer to the Symbolists than any other major Russian writer of his day. Chekhov's sea gull is not merely a bird, his cherry orchard a grove of trees, though the gull is visibly brought on stage dead, and the trees are audibly cut down. Both tenaciously cling, as Maeterlinck's symbols do not, to the real and supersede it. The great deficiency in Maeterlinck is that there is nothing to supersede, that his symbols are not anchored in reality.

Chekhov is not a realist: narrative and fact are not of supreme interest to him. He is not a formalist: he is not interested in methods meant to provide aesthetic pleasure. Character is his obsession, but what he means by character is different from what other writers mean. Psychology, yes; but he also sees characters as motifs, as repeated soundings of the same melody, as if they were subjects in a musical composition. *Remembrance of Things Past* and Chekhov's plays have this one thing in common: though conflicts of interest exist, it is the motif rather than dramatic tension that is the clue to structure.

Chekhov and James were the last great dramatizers of the unconscious. In Joyce and Proust, the unconscious comes into play on its own: in the interior monologue (Joyce) and the author's digressions on the action (Proust). Only Mann was interested in demonstrating abstract ideas in fiction. That is why the characters in *The Magic Mountain* suffer, why

Peeperkorn and Settembrini end up being merely mouthpieces. *The Magic Mountain* stands between two major styles, the realism of *Buddenbrooks* and the symbolism of *Death in Venice,* and lacks the perfection of both.

In *Death in Venice,* there are two characters who are essentially one—Aschenbach and Tadzio—and four minor characters who are also essentially one: the stranger in the cemetery; the old man on the boat; the gondolier; the singer in front of the hotel who smells of carbolic. They all have red hair, they all wear straw hats, and they all move in the same way.

A truly moral man, Chekhov detested morals.

What seems trivial at first in Chekhov's plays always turns out in the end to be the heart of the matter.

The mistake of people who still refer to Proust as a snob. Snobbery was a disease he cured himself of, but he described the symptoms so accurately that it is hard for certain readers to distinguish between the analysis of a former obsession and the obsession itself.

Scientist and writer both, Chekhov was unable to treat human life either clinically or sentimentally. Drawing on the two disciplines of his life, he became a kind of neurologist of fiction and the theater, who, in accurately describing the brain, in the name of truth included its dreams.

In a novel that turns on a moral crisis, the consciousness of the novelist should rarely be felt or not at all. James the great master. But in a novel whose very subject is consciousness, as in Proust, it should be felt everywhere.

Chekhov's symbols are either merely characteristic —Epihodov's billiards, Masha's snuff—or are at first characteristic and then become thematic—Nina's gull, Astrov's trees. Same thing happens in Faulkner's "That Evening Sun." The darkness refers both to the night and to the Negro. Nancy's fear of the dark, which is characteristic, will become the children's fear of Nancy's darkness, which is thematic.

Chapter headings for another book on Proust: 1 The Nature of Consciousness   2 The Screen of Habit   3 The Solution of Memory   4 The Illusion of Love   5 The Mask of Character   6 The Damnation of Time   7 The Triumph of Art

Remembrance of Things Past may be read as a philosophical drama in which no action occurs because the existence of character is finally disproved and the ideality of character made the only measure of reality.

The churches in Proust are important: *Remembrance of Things Past* can also be read as a religious book without a God.

The pleasures of Proust: When Odette walks in the Bois de Boulogne, the women's clothes and parasols turn into flowers.

In the scene at the opera, the theater is seen as society's ritual. The images are aquatic, marine, undersea. The passions, pretensions, and obsessions of the audience are mirrored back and forth between the beholder and the performer.

The aquarium image supersedes the garden image in Proust; Balbec, an aquarium, displaces Combray, a garden. Like the windows in Proust, the walls of the aquarium are both transparent and opaque. The narrator observes his own reflection as well as what his reflection is observing.

Leonie is a potentate and Françoise is her slave. In Leonie's bedroom, the court of Louis XIV is domesticated and narrowed down to two characters who perform its rituals.

The importance of the Jew and the homosexual in Proust: neither has a country of his own. Would *Remembrance of Things Past* be different if Proust had known of the coming existence of Israel or had read the Wolfenden Report?

The fine connections in Proust: The letter he waits for from Gilberte in *Within a Budding Grove* prepares for the scene in *Time Remembered* when he thinks he has received a telegram from Albertine long after her death. It is really from Gilberte. The irony of the scene is: the letter from Gilberte finally comes when he no longer cares. And the subtlety of it! It is because of an eccentricity in Gilberte's handwriting in the first volume of *Within a Budding Grove*—she makes her *G*'s like *A*'s—that this psychological error becomes plausible in *Time Remembered,* six volumes later.

Proust, the most tonal of all fiction writers, is also one of the most accurate. Imitations of Proust always go wrong in the same respect; they ape the tone but cannot duplicate the accuracy. There is no metaphor in the four thousand pages of Proust that is not precise. Proust's precision allows for any elaboration of style.

Rhetoric is a dirty word only when it is used to mask or ignore the truth. Shakespeare and Proust are rhetorical and truthful. The fear of rhetoric makes most modern writing dull. Reality is reduced to a kind of recipe book of facts in which categorical description becomes a substitute for perception. Novels that begin, "Lorinda hung her red, knitted blouse, which she had purchased at Macy's, on the hook on the green wall next to her unmade daybed, which Percy, her lover, who had gone to Harvard, had just left. . . ." are written by the thousands. Pseudofacts convince the reader, or are meant to, that he is being told the truth. Just as much a way of lying as fake rhetoric of novels that begin, "The evening was hazed over by a moth-like substance; the light, the wool of its temptation, blah blah . . ."

Chekhov's stories tread the finest line between a newspaper account and a fairy tale. Inferior writers step over the line one way or the other.

People Chekhov knew: Tolstoy, Gorki, Bunin, Tchaikowsky, Stanislavsky. Why is Tchaikowsky so surprising?

Proust destroyed the premises of fiction in the creation of a work of fiction. Proust creates identities only to say, "Since I have created these characters, I can definitely prove to you that they do not exist."

Three quotes from Chekhov:

". . . great writers and artists ought to engage in politics only to the extent necessary to defend themselves against politics. . . ."

"Subjectivity is a terrible thing . . . it reveals an author's hands and feet."

"One must not humiliate people—that is the chief thing."

Certain writers inspire affection in their readers that cannot be explained either by their work or by the facts of their lives. It proceeds from some temperamental undercurrent, some invisible connection between the writer and the reader that is more available to the senses and the emotions than to the mind. Bookish affections of this kind are deceptive and irrelevant, yet they truly exist. For me, Colette, Keats, and Chekhov inspire affection. Faulkner, Shelley, and Ibsen do not.

After one has read the work and the biographical studies of certain writers, they come to resemble composite versions of the characters they have invented:

Treplev and Trigorin in *The Sea Gull* seem like Chekhov, and Swann and Charlus like Proust.

Proust is a finer psychologist, Joyce a more daring innovator than Chekhov. It is tone alone that transforms Chekhov's stories into poems, the plays into music, even in translation. Ibsen is a great constructor but deficient in tone. Perhaps a language barrier in translation? Then why does the tone come through so clearly in Chekhov and Proust?

Tone is the most important quality of good writing and the hardest to define. It is not only a matter of relevance and consistency. Tone, a musical word, is essentially a matter of sound, rhythm, cadence, stress, and so on. Because all words are ultimately sounded, tone is that quality of writing which most approaches music and is therefore so difficult to pin down. But definable or not, it is crucial. Something like light in painting or timbre in music. It is that very quality in the use of words which is nonverbal, which does not depend on the *meaning* of the words alone—like the sound of a voice (tone of a voice), or the expression on a face while something is being said. It is what is meant, perhaps, by the phrase "between the lines." Something that is there but which cannot be pointed to specifically. Tone is like the color of water in a sea or a lake. As one takes up a handful to examine it, it disappears in the very process of being isolated and analyzed.

Sometimes there is a complete break in tone between one writer and another—Hopkins and Eliot, say—as there is in music between one composer and another. Debussy is the best example, I think. He must have sounded, originally, as if the history of music had not existed up to the point of his writing. A delusion, of course, but how could one relate him to Bach, Mozart, and Brahms without a great deal of special knowledge? There are, though, connecting links sometimes that are not immediately seen. Such as Turner and the Impressionists.

[1966]

Glenway Wescott
Love Birds of Prey

Glenway Wescott's short novel, *The Pilgrim Hawk*, has come out in a new edition, twenty-six years after it first appeared. Subtitled *A Love Story*, it is told in the first person by a narrator named Tower. Mr. Wescott's use of the first person is more than just one way of telling a story. What passes for a more or less objective account of events—more or less because Tower keeps questioning his own observations—boomerangs, and the tale leads us back to the teller. We believe in him as a character, but we become suspicious of his point of view. He reveals more than he knows, and what he reveals is himself, without seeming to be quite aware of it. We are dealing with two things at once: the story Tower tells and Tower's story. The effect is something like watching a movie whose main character turns out to be the cameraman.

The setting throughout *The Pilgrim Hawk* is a house and its garden in a French village; the action takes place in one afternoon. The classical unities of time and place are respected. The period is the twenties—the twenties being looked back at from the forties—and Mr. Wescott exploits that circumstance for two special purposes: love stories, in particular, are stories about time; by 1940, the France he is describing was on the point of no longer being free.

Three couples are on stage: Tower, a visiting American writer, and his friend and hostess Alexandra Henry, also American and owner of the French house; two servants, "a romantic pair named Eva and Jean," whom Alexandra has brought back from Morocco; and an expensive Irish couple, the Cullens, acquaintances of Alexandra's, who are passing through France on their way to a rented estate in Hungary. When Mrs. Cullen climbs out of her Daimler onto the cobblestoned square that separates Alexandra's house from a highway, it is "a delicate operation, for she bore a full-grown hooded falcon on her wrist. A dapper young chauffeur also helped." The hawk and the chauffeur, whose name is Ricketts, appropriately make their entrance at the same time, for the hawk is to become the symbol of, the chauffeur a fulcrum for, love's troubles and delusions. The three couples become involved in a series of triangles before the afternoon is over. Two of the triangles are examined for our benefit by the narrator: the Cullens and the hawk; the servants and the chauffeur. But there is a third, of which Tower is a member, that we must discover for ourselves, and part of the impact of *The Pilgrim Hawk* is the result of our uneasy awareness of this triangle's existence.

As the afternoon wears on, the Cullens reveal themselves to be more eccentric, more complicated than we first imagined. The antagonism between them, revolving ostensibly around the hawk—the wife cherishes it, the husband loathes it—is sexual, petulant, and destructive. Murderers-admirers, the Cullens have not succeeded in domesticating each other, in killing each other, or in freeing themselves. They are forever perched between slavery and flight—human versions of Mrs. Cullen's pilgrim hawk, which, enslaved by an appetite described as the most intense in nature, will as an individual trade its freedom for food but has remained wild as a species for over forty centuries. This half-state of the Cullens—a cultivated wildness—is their particular milieu; they are hunters wandering across the face of the world, killers under the sheen of money and manners.

Alexandra invites the Cullens to stay to dinner. They accept. Alexandra and her guests go for a walk in the park beyond her garden, but the two couples return separately. The hawk is fed, dinner is being prepared (a casserole of pigeons, one of which has been fed to the hawk). Mrs. Cullen tethers the hawk to a bench in the garden, and the two women temporarily retire. Mr. Cullen gets drunk—or pretends to—and discusses his marriage with Tower. Then Tower goes out to the kitchen to check up on the dinner preparations and happens to look out the window. He sees Cullen stealthily approach the hawk, unhood it, and cut its leash with a penknife. Two events occur: a jealous quarrel in the kitchen involving Eva, Jean, and Ricketts; the recapture of the hawk by Mrs. Cullen, who does not accuse Cullen of releasing it, though she is obviously aware of the fact. The Cullens abruptly

decide to leave without dinner, the excuse being a
phone call Mrs. Cullen puts through to her brother
in Paris, where something has gone wrong. The Cullens depart. A moment later, the Daimler narrowly
escapes crashing into a car on the highway. Mrs. Cullen
returns alone, agitated, the hawk still fastened to her
wrist, and a revolver in one hand. Cullen, she says,
had threatened to use it as they drove away. But on
whom she is not sure. Herself or Ricketts? It does not
occur to her, as it does to Alexandra, that Cullen might
have intended it for himself. It does not occur to Alexandra, as it does to Tower, that Mrs. Cullen might have
intended it for *her*self. She throws the revolver into the
garden pond, makes her embarrassed apologies, and
finally takes her leave. There is a kind of small coda
to the novel: Alexandra and Tower briefly and lightly
refer to the events of the afternoon.

The Pilgrim Hawk poses the captive against the
free, and finding only an armed truce between them,
questions the definitions of both. There are no easy
definitions, it turns out; they are endlessly definable.
To be free—in humans—means being neither wild nor
captured. The balance is very fine, for sometimes to
allow oneself to be captured is a mark of freedom,
and what we take to be freedom a form of captivity.
Jean and Eva and the Cullens play—childishly or dan-
gerously—the game of liberty-capture. The narrator,
the watcher, is at times the chorus, at times a Machia-
vellian, perhaps, complicitor; it is he who gets Cullen drunk, he who tells Mrs. Cullen the hawk has got
free. And he seems overconcerned about the effect the

Cullens's behavior will have on Alexandra. Will it damage her attitude toward love? Toward marriage? He
is avuncular, not sexual. At least not here. Moreover,
as we listen to his voice, he is extraordinarily concerned
with his own reactions. As he slowly uncovers the self-
interest and narcissism of the Cullens, we begin to
taste the flavor of his own—sometimes self-deprecatory,
sometimes flattering, always obsessively doubtful. Our
narrator has a relationship with himself, and anyone
who gets involved with him, we feel, may find two
parts of a triangle already there. He is a writer, a preda-
tory hawk of another kind, but has missed the quarry in
life—not self-sufficient enough to be free, not driven
enough to give up the idea of freedom for captivity.
He, too, is on a perch, and knows something of the
meaning of a bloodstained gauntlet—the luring jail
of Mrs. Cullen's leather glove, on which the hawk
lives out its life. When a falconer releases a captive
pilgrim hawk to feed, it cannot miss its quarry more
than twice; if it misses three times, it may attempt to
go free. If it does, there's a good chance of its starving
to death. Tower, we learn, has been a two-time loser
in love. When Cullen lets the hawk go, it flies away,
but not far—not yet. Appetite has committed it to
bondage, just as their natures have doomed the Cullens
and Tower to one form of enslavement, one form of
hawkhood or another.

Madness, love, art, death—the hawk is compared to
all these things in turn as the afternoon wears on and it
is seen from different angles, and differently. Almost
every fact and insight in *The Pilgrim Hawk* is looked
at twice. The unfolding drama is a little relay race

between the apparent and the real. Mrs. Cullen tells
us first that she and her husband have left Ireland because she cannot bear to ride a horse anyone else
mounts. Her sons have appropriated her horses. Later,
she tells us the real reason: Cullen drinks too much
and is a bad example for her sons. But *is* it the real
reason? By the time Cullen tells Tower of the merry
chase his wife has led him around the world, of her
whims, her irrationalities, we are not sure. And at the
end, there is another turn of the screw; it is Cullen
we see as the problem, Mrs. Cullen as the put-upon
protector. Similarly, a tear-stricken Eva, afraid that
Jean is going to kill her because she has flirted with
Ricketts, explains to Tower and Alexandra that she
flirts only so that Jean's love for her can be made mani-
fest over and over again—a need of Jean's as much as it
is hers. Jealousy is the necessary oxygen of their emotions; what she appears to do against Jean she is really
doing for him. And to Tower, what is evident at one
moment becomes suspect the next. His view of life becomes our view of him. The whole afternoon seems to
take place in a transparent globe, variously lit, turning
slowly but steadily. The reader is constantly being re-
positioned, constantly being forced to see something he
didn't quite see before. Mr. Wescott's world is self-
contained but precarious, and, like the real one, endlessly full of meaning. We are given not one choice
but many in interpreting what occurs.

Yet the major theme is clear: "When love is at stake,
love of liberty is as a rule only fear of captivity." The
irony is that the wildest of passions must lead to some
form of domestication; freedom and dependence are

not as reconcilable as we like to pretend. The true insight of *The Pilgrim Hawk* is that freedom and bondage can become cravings, and, in the end, the same thing precisely because they *are* cravings. Cullen who detests the hawk—his rival, his embarrassment, his other nature—is the most illustrative. He has attempted to get rid of the hawk. Here he is watching his wife's attempt to rescue it:

> Only Cullen was deathly still, not even puffing. I moved far enough away from him to see his face, and found there, added to the bibulous pink, a pale light of wild relief, reprieve, even rapture, as if that horrid bird on his wife's arm returning to haunt him again had been his heart's desire.

Mrs. Cullen's image changes drastically in the few hours of the novel's action from a fashionable, worldly woman (the narrator's original view) to a proud young Dublin beauty (Cullen's original view), and ultimately into a kind of earth mother, a powerful figure whose muscled back and peasant stance contrast sharply with the slim ankle Tower glimpses through a silk stocking at the beginning of the novel. Cullen is two-sided, at least—a greedy man-boy Irishman, and the frustrated, dangerous killer he may become. Even here, ambiguity, rather than clouding the issue, turns it around. Is Mrs. Cullen getting rid of the gun as she plans to get rid of Ricketts, because she does not wish to be tempted to violence herself? But again, as in the case of Cullen, who would her target be? Cullen because of the hawk? Ricketts because of Eva? The Cullens being hawks and their quarry each other, the hunter and the hunted keep changing places. Jean and Eva, a backstairs counterpart of the action taking place in the drawing room, are more innocent, more adolescent. Still, their petty jealousies may develop into the concentrated poison that infects the Cullens. Ricketts, the third in the kitchen triangle, is possibly part of the Cullens's drawing room triangle, too. Cullen hints as much several times, and something similar has happened before; out of jealousy, Cullen once threatened an Irish poet with a knife. Ricketts's relationship to Mrs. Cullen is uncertain; the implications are left hanging. Significantly, Mrs. Cullen twice talks of getting rid of Ricketts, as if she had forgotten the subject had already been mentioned.

Appetite, gustatory and sexual, weighs heavily on the atmosphere of *The Pilgrim Hawk* and pollutes the air. It is the air, the novel implies, we all breathe. As for love:

> Unrequited passion; romance put asunder by circumstances or mistakes; sexuality pretending to be love—all that is a matter of little consequence, a mere voluntary temporary uneasiness, compared with the long course of true love, especially marriage. In marriage, insult arises again and again and again; and pain has not only to be endured, but consented to; and the amount of forgiveness that it necessitates is incredible and exhausting. When love has given satisfaction, then you discover how large a part of the rest of life is only payment for it, installment after installment.

The Cullens dread and promote the worst situation

in love: to be the third person in a triangle. The real or
imagined existence of a rival perpetuates and exacer-
bates their marriage, for it keeps interest alive while it
arouses and deflects hatred. Cullen's enemy is the hawk,
not Mrs. Cullen, or so he must, or chooses to, believe.
At one point, he admits to Tower that he is envious of
the kind of life Alexandra and Tower seem to be leading—a harmless, peaceful domesticity; it has no hawk
in it. But that is precisely what is wrong with Alexandra and Tower's relationship. The narrator, so keen
on protecting Alexandra from predators, is not really
so enviable. There is a fate as terrible as being third,
and that is not even to be third, to be on the outside
looking in, prey to the cruelties of sexual passion, but
prey to them vicariously. It is a voyeurism familiar
to artists drawing from life—in this case the narrator-
writer. And it may be why we see both the release and
the recapture of the hawk at a distance, through a
window. Yet Tower's position is paradoxical; without
him, we would know nothing of all this. And as if to
reinforce the point of vicariousness, the power of viewpoint, an afterthought surfaces up to us at the very end
of the novel. The Cullens have left; dinner is over.
Alexandra and Tower are alone:

> "You'll never marry, dear," I said to tease Alex.
> "Your friend Mrs. Cullen thinks you will, but she
> has no imagination. You'll be afraid to, after this
> fantastic bad luck."
> "What bad luck, if you please?" she inquired,
> smiling to show that my mockery was welcome.
> "Fantastic bad object lessons."

"You're no novelist," she said, to tease me. "I envy the Cullens, didn't you know?" And I concluded from the look on her face that she herself did not quite know whether she meant it.

The End. But there is something tantalizing here, something enigmatic. We can't quite dredge the solution up to consciousness. What are Alexandra and Tower doing in this novel of couples and triangles? They are not really a couple, not parts of a triangle.

Or are they? Just as the narrator must have searched his memory to recapture this one afternoon so marvelously re-created for us, we search ours, and it comes to us at last. Ah! A fact we had forgotten, planted in the last line of the very first paragraph: "That was in May of 1928 or 1929, before we all returned to America, and she [Alexandra] met my brother and married him."

So Alexandra does marry, after all, and she marries . . . *is* married . . . very close to home.

[1967]

Dylan Thomas
A Thin, Curly
Little Person

In an early letter to Pamela Hansford Johnson in *Selected Letters of Dylan Thomas,* Thomas explains his ideas about poetry. It is a letter from one aspiring young poet to another. Miss Johnson and Thomas had not yet met. Thomas was nineteen.

Nearly all my images [come] from my solid and fluid world of flesh and blood. . . . To contrast a superficial beauty with a superficial ugliness, I do not contrast a tree with a pylon, or a bird with a weazel, but rather the human limbs with the human tripes. . . . Only by association is the refuse of the body more to be abhorred than the body itself. . . . All thoughts and actions emanate from the body. Every idea, intuitive or intellectual, can be imaged and translated in terms of the body, its flesh, skin, blood, sinews, veins, glands, organs, cells, or senses.

Here is Thomas on himself, at the same age, again writing to Miss Johnson:

Don't expect too much of me (it's conceit to suppose that you would); I'm an odd little person. Don't imagine the great jawed writer brooding over his latest masterpiece in the oak study, but a thin, curly little person, smoking too many cigarettes, with a crocked lung, and writing his vague verses in the back room of a provincial villa. . . . I am not a particular nuisance, and I smell quite nice. I look about fourteen, and I have a large, round nose; nature gave it to me, but fate, and a weak banister, broke it; in cold weather, it is sufficiently glossy to light up my room. When I am about on winter nights there is no need for the gas. Cough! cough! cough! my death is marching on. . . .

The difference in tone between Thomas theorizing about poetry and Thomas describing himself is not a difference in theme. A split between his notion of the body as a metaphor and the dim view he took of himself as a person always existed, and, as the years went by, it widened. What started out as a charming diffidence ended up as serious self-accusation. Like his feeling for Wales—often hated when he was there and longed for when he was not—his attitude toward the body pivoted ambiguously. Because he held the body in such awe, his own did not delight him. It was the only one he had. As a poet, Thomas was not interested in the institutions of the world and relied on an organic unity between himself and a landscape conceived in biological terms. More than most poets, he was, therefore, his own universe. What he was most committed to were the poems. He increasingly came to dislike not their subject but their source.

The split wasn't helped by two obvious stumbling blocks: a lack of money and a need for alcohol. Thomas's father was a schoolteacher, and the Welsh town of Swansea, where Thomas spent the first nineteen years of his life, was not opulent. Poverty became a really grim fact when Thomas married, fathered a family, and tried to settle into some sort of permanent home. The move to the Boat House at Laugharne, the place most associated with his life and work, was made in 1949, when he was thirty-four. In between Swansea and Laugharne, he lived in London, Hampshire, Wilshire, Cardiganshire, and Oxford. For a person rooted in a particular place for most of his life, a later lack of stability and need for money can be especially excruciating. Yet it would be impossible to say that Thomas drank because of outside pressure. Here he is at seventeen, a newspaper reporter on the *South Wales Evening Post* and an amateur actor playing in *Hay Fever*:

> Much of my time is taken up with rehearsals. Much is taken up with concerts, deaths, meetings and dinners. It's odd, but between all these I manage to become drunk at least four nights a week. . . . It's a Sunday morning; I've got a head like a wind-mill.

At eighteen:

> I have a villain of a headache, my eyes are two

piss-holes in the sand, my tongue is fish-and-chip
paper. . . . It is difficult to write, because the
bending of the head hurts like fury. And my
hand ain't what she was.

Thomas occasionally escaped from the condition of
poverty, but never from the sense of it; alcohol became increasingly inescapable.

But the gulf between Thomas the poet and
Thomas everything else—reporter, actor, novelist,
film writer, playwright, lecturer, short-story writer—
rather than being divisive was one of the signs of his
hold on life. He knew from the beginning just what
kind of poet he wanted to be and was.

I have been writing since I was a very little boy,
and have always been struggling with the same
things, with the idea of poetry as a thing entirely
removed from such accomplishments as "word-
painting," and the setting down of delicate but
usual emotions in a few, well-chosen words. . . .
there is always the one right word: use it, despite
its foul or merely ludicrous associations. . . . It is
part of a poet's job to take a debauched and pros-
tituted word, like the beautiful word, "blond,"
and to smooth away the lines of its dissipation,
and to put it on the market again, fresh and virgin. . . . [The artist] is a law unto himself, and
. . . has only one limitation, and that is the
widest of all: the limitation of form. Poetry finds
its own form; form should never be superim-
posed; the structure should rise out of the words
and the expression of them. I do not want to ex-

press what other people have felt; I want to rip something away and show what they have never seen. . . .

Thomas, who could write almost anything, kept the idea and the practice of poetry sacrosanct. A natural light verse writer—the letters are full of enviable examples—he published none, wrote few occasional pieces, and the poems, though they decrease in quantity, show no falling off of pitch or intensity. Thomas remained whole as a poet without compromise, though he may have had to compromise almost everything else to do so. The letters reveal two essential facts: his most productive period as a poet came between the ages of sixteen and twenty; his absolute refusal to allow the journalist, entertainer, and comedian a foothold in the poems. The decision to separate the obvious talent from the chancy genius was made early.

The baneful self-absorption, the adolescent miseries of the early letters are commonplace. Their intelligence and humor are not. What is rare is the quality of the writing—almost everywhere so remarkable, so natural that, in the end, the letters, rather than Thomas's published prose, make his second greatest claim to genius after the poems. No biography can touch them in immediacy, and nowhere else is Thomas so mordantly funny. In the letters, a personality unfamiliar to the poems makes his most spectacular appearance: the childlike but knowledgeable observer-storyteller with an inexhaustible verbal imagination.

But two notes struck early, little chimes we try not to hear, become peals: guilt and self-disgust. The whining after money is real and terrible enough. At one point, Thomas had a wife and three children to support, no means of income, and the worry of a sick mother and a dying father living on a small pension. In spite of the cold fact of poverty, the apologies, the self-torturing explanations of why he did not get to where he was supposed to be, of why he did not do what he was supposed to do finally make a psychological point. Thomas was a dependent person who took on enormous responsibilities he couldn't handle, and there is a kind of childlike insistence on being taken care of which, when thwarted, threatens *him*. Self-defeat stamps the letters like a watermark. It is not finally avoidable as a symptom. Recognition was no problem; it came almost immediately. Money did not come with it. That Thomas should have had to mooch his way through film scripts and BBC broadcasts, to depend on patrons to scrape out a living, is deplorable but not unusual. Other poets were and are in the same boat. What is peculiar is not taking on and relinquishing responsibility, or playing out the role of the roaring boy drunk—two typical versions of how poets behave—but the inability to distinguish between the important claim and the peripheral one in a person who is able to distinguish so much. That may have been one way of safeguarding the poems, the most important claim of all. Often, the confusions of drink seem just as likely an explanation.

Drunkenness kept Thomas endlessly open to further apologies and deeper self-disgust. Extremely

aware of sham and pretense, he took a very poor view
of his own, and his ability to act was weakened by
his insight. Emotionally a provincial, he was in every
other sense extraordinarily worldly. In fact, part of
the charm of his conversation and of these letters is
the odd mixture of the adolescent and the wise man,
of someone who seems to know exactly what the
world is like, only to fall short of dealing with it,
time after time. That defect eventually became a virtue to a large audience, which was awed by his accomplishment and allowed to feel compassionate
about his personal life. The "Dylan Thomas legend"
was built on that double standard. A spellbinder with
a fine comic sense of life's absurdity, the mind and
vocabulary of a great poet, and no official armor is a
luring combination, especially when it is made so
publicly available. Thomas kept literally giving himself away, counting on a reserve that was pure energy
sparked by alcohol. Nothing is more attractive than
ironic despair to an audience who can enjoy the irony
without having to pay for the despair.

Thomas was supremely intelligent but not an intellectual, and abstract concepts get short shrift in
the letters. That is not true of ideas, and he is fascinating on everything he touches with the exception
of politics, on which he is simple-minded and murky.
He is particularly good on the craft of poetry, the dis-
section of character, the random incident, and landscape. The virtuosity of Thomas's language is hypnotic
—an extra dividend whenever he is talking about the
arts, because his opinions are so sound. Even when

there is a certain brash exaggeration in his judgments, they are never without truth. Here he is, for instance, on Wagner:

> Wagner moves me, too, but much in the same way as the final spectacular scene in a pantomime. I won't deny, for a moment, that he's a great composer, but his greatness lies in girth rather than in depth; it lacks humour and subtlety; he creates everything for you in a vast Cecil de Mille way; his orchestration is a perpetual "close-up"; there is altogether too much showmanship and exhibitionism about him. His Valhalla is a very large and a very splendid place, but built in the style of a German baronial castle; the tapestries are too voluminous & highly coloured, there is too great a display of gold; while the gods that hold dominion over it are florid deities, puffed out with self-importance, wearing gaudy garments and angelic watch-chains. . . . he reminds me of a huge and overblown profiteer, wallowing in fineries, overexhibiting his monstrous paunch and purse, and drowning his ten-ton wife in a great orgy of jewels. Compare him to an aristocrat like Bach!

Thomas believed that "a born writer is born scrofulous; his career is an accident dictated by physical or circumstantial disabilities." The least attractive motif in the letters—the begging and wheedling—suggests a disability beyond necessity. Something determined or compulsive seems to have lurked behind his difficulties in handling money, in meeting commitments, in living up to promises—perhaps some rebellion in which failure was a more viable criticism of the world he found himself in than success. Thomas saw too much about which there was nothing to do. Independence and success may have meant giving up some version of childhood on which the poems depended, and joining the enemy. Thomas never did. He remained true to the person he basically was. Or perhaps it was only by trying to make himself small that he could fit his odd largeness into a world that had no particular pigeonhole to accommodate his particular pigeon. Unlike all poets, he was kind; but like most poets, he was nervous, thin-skinned, and not adaptable.

Often in Thomas's conversation, one could hear a somewhat different tune than the words implied orchestrating them somewhere off in the distance. The letters have something of the same effect. Priceless as a record, wonderful to read, they are, as a whole, finally chilling. We are enchanted. We are charmed. It takes some time to realize that what we are being charmed into is a nightmare—the history of a wildly gifted and brilliant child, not only stumbling and bumbling his way to the grave, but digging it for himself in the process.

[1967]

Lois Moyles
An Introduction

The first thing to say about Miss Moyles's poems is: she writes like no one else. The worlds created in these poems are her own, and singular, but they transcend the personal not only by bearing resemblances to worlds we know but by having an unmistakable authority of their own. They are new, but they are not eccentric and they are not ignorable. Reading them, a kind of osmosis takes place; they bring up —in their way of imagining things, in their facts and phantasies—a real world we are familiar with, and they enrich it, as it enriches them, by transferring meanings, images, ideas, one to the other. It is as if a fine-skinned cell were transferring nourishments and wastes, each the necessary partner to the other.

These poems depend largely on three things: a tone of voice (not heard before, I believe); the nature of their images; and, most surprisingly, drama. They are, in a very special sense, dramatic poems; they have suspense, and, in each, a situation somehow endangers its characters—its "I" or "we"—until it is resolved. To say exactly what these situations are would be dangerous. They are just under the skin and into the dark, but what they bring back from wherever they go is real blood, and real light. They do what I think the best poems do; they let you know without your being quite able to say what or how.

The freshness of the poems is twofold: their language and the connections they make. For instance, in "My Innocence," the connection between virginity and coins—meaningful in the poem, and meaningful, later, as an abstract idea worth thinking about. It is a poem about time; Miss Moyles has seen a connection between time and money that has escaped almost everyone else. Or, to take the beginning of "Once Like Adam": to think of anyone as having thirteen hundred bones is a gift Miss Moyles gives us. It is a truth; it also enlarges the imagination. Certain preoccupations and words reappear: *face, side, body,* and so on. But they are used in the service of new insights: "It no longer escapes me / that it was to vanish my innocence came here . . ." I don't think anyone else has quite noticed or said that innocence becomes known by its having to be lost. And if one looks twice at the phrase, "It no longer escapes me," another shade of meaning appears. I think Miss Moyles suggests not only the usual connotations of "It no longer escapes me," but a further one: innocence, once lost, is no longer there *to* escape. And in the play of meanings between "vanish" and "came here," innocence is not seen in its usual guise, as passive, acted upon. Here, innocence arrives somewhere for the express purpose of vanishing. It is either born to do so, compelled to do so, or insistent upon doing so. Miss Moyles can be either spare or rich; she is always subtle, and I mention these possibilities to suggest her way of doing things.

To a poet, where one starts out is of vital importance; yet it is never quite as important as where one ends up. In "For the Wars," to take an example, Miss Moyles starts out with a California heiress. By the time she finishes, she has managed to ring imperial changes on the great themes of war and peace. The connection between the heiress and the stock market, guerrillas, Quakers, generals, parades, orators, judges, merchant fleets, statues, guards, inventors, purse strings, and, finally, "trucks / filled with soft brown stores / for the wars" is not lost on us. Or shouldn't be. And what might have been merely a portrait in other hands has widened into a poem whose implications have moved from its ostensible subject to its subject's many objects. What I'm trying to suggest here is that it is not enough to say something in a new way. One has to have something new to say, and Miss Moyles has it.

"For the Wars" is somewhat different from earlier poems in having a more open texture, a freer range of associations. Miss Moyles is very good in tight moments, where she can work with speed and vitality while still adhering to close rhymes. She has never been a "formal" poet in this sense, but I think the following lines from a poem not printed here, "A Tale Told By a Head," show what she can do in this vein:

> A nature walk was a kind of
> Belgian bestiary brought with me

> where one tapestried foot at a time
>   was woven to the ground,
> where my hounds followed face down
> like surface swimmers unable to drown . . .

These poems are original. Many people write original poems—or at least one or two of them. But Miss Moyles is doing something else, too, and something more. She is being consistent, for a way of looking at the world finally emerges from these poems; it refreshes the world by what it sees as well as by its way of seeing. Most important of all, these poems are natural. We are overhearing the real voice—and not some literary counterpart—of another human being. That that voice should happen to belong to a poet as talented as Miss Moyles is lucky. Lucky for her, of course —but I think even luckier for us.

[1967]

A Contribution
to a Symposium

"We invite you to submit a written statement, formal or informal, in which you may tell us what you are doing, what you think other poets are doing, what real difference—if any—there is between your poetry and that of the previous generation, what technical devices you are using, what kind of subject matter you think is most pertinent to poetry in the 1960's, or anything else which concerns the poetry that is being written now."

From a letter from *South Dakota Review*

1: A reaction has obviously set in against the "formal" poem—that is, one closely rhymed, or rhymed at all, strictly metrical, and so on. This seems to me both good and bad. Good insofar as it is an attempt to avoid lying, artifice, and fitting things together that do not really belong. Bad insofar as it mistakes technique for form and condemns, out of hand and theoretically, what might be good in fact. Good poems are being written that use tight formal structures. Larkin is an example in England, Merrill is an example here. Good poems are being written that do not use tight formal structures. Hughes is an example in England, Merwin is an example here. The problem of how to write a poem and still be natural has become crucial. Elizabeth Bishop is, I think, the first American poet who saw that the conversational, the tone and rhythm of speech, could be used *within* a formal structure, rather than requiring the poet to dispense with formal structure entirely.

2: The image, central to any kind of poetry, is receiving more attention in and of itself. I mean as distinct from syntax. Certain Spanish and South American poets, such as Lorca, Neruda, Andrade, etc. have become major influences. The trouble with this, often, is that the banalities of English meter and rhyme are exchanged for the banalities of poems based frequently on English *translations* of Spanish.

3: The idea of an American poetry as distinct from a British poetry is an important critical idea, but an idea that's becoming more hidebound than I think Williams ever intended. He saw and could appreciate the advantages of Stevens. The idea that one should write as one speaks is attractive but it easily leads to parochialism—and prose. Though no one could deny that languages are different, poetry is international, not American or British. It is true, though, that the problem is special. American and British English seem the same language, and Americans were brought up on British poetry, not the other way around. So there is a kind of overreactiveness to anything that smacks of the

British-literary. The same kind of reaction would not, I think, be a problem to a French poet, say, reading an Italian poet. There is a real objection to a national poetry, whether it's American, Italian, or Russian. The very notion of it presupposes some sort of moral stricture. A word like *elegance* has become pejorative when, actually, there is nothing pejorative about elegance. In short: what started out as an attack on the literary and academic has somehow ended up as a forbidding touchstone. Originality and importance are not national but individual.

4: Because of the split between "raw" and "cooked" poetry—Lowell's words, originally, I believe—cliques have developed, just as they have in painting and in music. The chief weapon of the literary politician is to put a poet in a pigeonhole. The poet has to spend so much time defending himself against the classification that he hardly has time to write. That knocks him out as competition for a couple of years. The whole picture of poets as dealers in reputations is degrading. "Schools" of poetry, insistences on the way to write or not to write are deadening. All breast beaters and theoreticians should be avoided like the plague. Nothing is more depressing than to see a group set out to counterbalance what they think is the Establishment and become as boring as what they set out to supplant.

5: Poems can't be written by everybody. The idea that they can has always existed. Because the standards no longer involve craft in any traditional sense, the distinction between naturalness, which is admirable, and ignorance, which is not, has become blurred. A lot of people no longer write sestinas so boring they drop from your hand. But, instead, a lot of people write grocery lists so boring that sometimes you wish you could get your hands on a sestina. Poetry is still an art. The idea that it is not is comforting to people who are not poets and meaningless to people who are. It is not ignorance that defeats academicism but talent. Development is a product of talent. Without talent, you get nothing. Without development, you may get a poem or two, but you don't get a poet.

[1967]

Flann O'Brien
Tom Swift in Hell

The nameless narrator and chief character of Flann O'Brien's *The Third Policeman* dies in the course of the action, but we do not know it at the time. It comes as a surprise, and yet is plausible in retrospect—a flash of light at the end of the tunnel by which we can retrace our route. It is not an easy route to follow, forward or back: the landscape is bizarre, the events have the cliff-hanging aspects of a boy's adventure story as well as the frightening conviction of a nightmare, and time is distorted. The three days that pass in the narrator's life, or death, turn out to be twenty years for his hired hand, John Divney, and an eternity for three policemen—Policeman Fox, the third policeman of the novel's title, and his two colleagues, Sergeant Pluck and Policeman MacCruiskeen.

Starting out as a realistic novel, *The Third Policeman* rapidly changes into a book of magic deeds and transformations. Divney and the narrator kill a rich old man, Phillip Mathers, in order to get their hands on a black box containing three thousand pounds. The narrator is finishing Mathers off with a spade when Divney disappears, taking the black box with him; he returns, empty-handed, a few moments later. He eludes the narrator's questions about its whereabouts for months, then finally leads him to Mathers's house, where the box has been hidden under the floorboards. Divney remains outside, and the narrator enters the house, but when he reaches in under the floorboards to get the box, it slips out of his hands. (We learn later that Divney has substituted explosives for the pounds.) Immediately, the narrator becomes aware of Mathers's presence in the room—a ghost, the narrator thinks, though, unknown to himself and the reader, he is now a ghost himself.

During a conversation between Mathers and the narrator, a third character speaks up—the narrator's soul, called Joe, who provides an intermittent, subterranean commentary on the narrator's behavior from then on. Complicity in Mathers's murder leads the narrator to a kind of hell dominated by a surrealistic police barracks —one-dimensional from one point of view, three-dimensional from another—which is the governing center of a countryside populated by people who are in part bicycles. An exchange of atoms between a cyclist and his machine produces various percentages of man-bike or bike-man, and it is one of the chief tasks of the policemen to keep track of the percentages from moment to moment. (Sergeant Pluck, whose main activity is the recovery of stolen bicycles, actually steals them himself.) A scaffold is built for the narrator's execution, which never takes place. He is led down a secret road

by Pluck and MacCruiskeen to an underground structure—"eternity," a complex of repeated rooms, wires,
mechanisms, and lights. It has a weighing machine, an
elevator, and bank vaults from which any object of desire can be released for the asking—but only to be seen
and handled, not removed. To exit from "eternity,"
one must weigh what he weighed when he entered it;
it is a place of wish fulfillment and disappointment.
Time has stopped in "eternity." Cigarettes, though
smoked, remain the same length; the outside world
stays exactly as it was—a jammed movie frame—during
the narrator's underground sojourn. The policemen's
world is one of tantalizing nonsense and disruptive
shocks—a world in which science and magic have got
mixed up and horrible fates are narrowly escaped time
after time.

Joe is not O'Brien's only means of digressing from
the action in order to throw light on it; his most successful creation is a dead physicist-philosopher, De
Selby, about whose life and work the narrator is com-
piling an index. In fact, it is for the sake of the De
Selby index that he is lured into murder by Divney,
who robs him of his farm and pub, and, eventually,
his life—the last-minute revelation in the novel that
jiggles its enigmatic patterns into a meaningful whole.
De Selby is presented to us, most often in footnotes,
as a scientific genius with theories about everything
imaginable: houses, roads, journeys, hammering, water,
and so on. Along with De Selby comes an army of De
Selby specialists—historians, biographers, and scientists,
such as the Englishmen, Hatchjaw and Bassett; a Swiss,

Le Clerque; a mocking Frenchman, Du Grabandier, whose attacks on De Selby are often answered by a shadowy German named Kraus. Kraus is, on the weight of the evidence, merely Du Grabandier in disguise, rushing back and forth between Hamburg and Paris. There are others, including Henderson, an explicator not of De Selby but of Hatchjaw and Bassett. One could easily imagine a commentator on Henderson commenting on Hatchjaw and Bassett commenting on De Selby—a phenomenon familiar to scholarship and similar to the parallel mirrors that repeat images to infinity (which De Selby arranges for one of his experiments) or to the chest that contains exact but successively smaller reproductions of itself to the point of intangibility (a creation of Policeman MacCruiskeen, who works on his miniature models with invisible tools).

O'Brien's finest moments involve De Selby and the crew of indefatigable scribblers who have devoted their lives to his theories. The footnotes change, like so many things in *The Third Policeman,* from a credible literalness at the beginning of the book into an absurd hodgepodge of contradiction as we pursue the clues to De Selby's—*and* the narrator's—existence and identity. The narrator's deadpan sobriety in dealing with De Selby in the peculiar language of pedantry is as revealing in unmasking the genius as a crank as the actual content of De Selby's theories:

[1] Not excepting even the credulous Kraus (see his *De Selbys Leben*), all the commentators have

treated De Selby's disquisitions on night and sleep with considerable reserve. This is hardly to be wondered at since he held (a) that darkness is simply an accretion of "black air," i.e., a staining of the atmosphere due to volcanic eruptions too fine to be seen with the naked eye and also to certain "regrettable" industrial activities involving coal-tar by-products and vegetable dyes; and (b) that sleep was simply a succession of fainting-fits brought on by semi-consciousness due to (a). Hatchjaw brings forward his rather facile and ever-ready theory of forgery, pointing to certain unfamiliar syntactical constructions in the first part of the so-called "prosecanto" in *Golden Hours*. He does not, however, suggest that there is anything spurious in De Selby's equally damaging rhodomontade in the *Layman's Atlas* where he inveighs savagely against "the insanitary conditions prevailing everywhere after six o'clock" and makes the famous *gaffe* that death is merely "the collapse of the heart from the strain of a lifetime of fits and fainting." Bassett (in *Lux Mundi*) has gone to considerable pains to establish the date of these passages and shows that De Selby was *hors de combat* from his long-standing gall-bladder disorders at least immediately before the passages were composed. One cannot lightly set aside Bassett's formidable table of dates and his corroborative extracts from contemporary newspapers which treat of an unnamed "elderly man" being assisted into private houses after having fits in the street. For those who wish to hold the balance for themselves,

Henderson's *Hatchjaw and Bassett* is not unuseful. Kraus, usually unscientific and unreliable, is worth reading on this point. (*Leben,* pp. 17–37.)

Gradually, we come to realize that the De Selby footnotes are not merely fancy fingerwork, O'Brien's little joke, but a series of clues to the very heart of the matter. De Selby's test-tube universe, a pastiche of half-fact and half-fiction, is not very different from the pseudo-scientific and fantastic world in which the narrator finds himself. Both are strange to the reader but real to their respective protagonists. Our narrator is hellish to begin with; he has a wooden leg and is crippled, he has no name and no identity, and desire, sex, and love never concern him in the least. (Footnote: One of De Selby's many peculiar attributes is his inability to distinguish one sex from the other.) Human relationships in *The Third Policeman* are limited to those of plotter and complicitor, murderer and victim, executioner and condemned—each a distorted mirror image of the other, like the narrator and De Selby. De Selby is finally unmasked as a comic fraud; it is through the narrator's very interest in De Selby that the person we first take to be a scholar finally becomes known to us as a schoolboy and a dud.

Just as MacCruiskeen's chest keeps repeating itself, so one of O'Brien's major devices is doubling, or tripling—he is writing a "Chinese box" of a novel, in which appearances are not what they seem and each image is pregnant with another. The black box first contains money, then explosives, and finally "omnium," a source of energy from which, we are told, all the action

and magic of the novel proceed; the narrator contains
Joe, his soul; a *second* police barracks, the domain of Policeman Fox, is built *inside* the walls of Mathers's house;
in eternity, there is an actual place called "eternity";
Du Grabandier contains Kraus; the vaults of "eternity"
contain the objects of our wishes, never to be possessed.
The images of boxes, barracks, chests, and underground
rooms recur, and we begin to associate the idea of
enclosure, of containment and confinement, with the
idea of hell—an idea in sharp contrast to O'Brien's open
and fresh descriptions of the natural world. Ultimately,
the narrator's death contains his life, or—if we read
O'Brien's book for its counterpoint rather than for its
ostensible theme—his life embodies his death. At the
end of the novel, he stands on the threshold of the police
barracks once more, this time with Divney, who has
died of a heart attack, beside him. Repeating the exact
words he has used to describe the narrator's first arrival
at the barracks, O'Brien lets us know that the action
of the novel is about to unwind itself again, ad infi-
nitum.

The Third Policeman is a comic but sinister invention: a regional farce in which a criminal struggles
with an entrenched rural bureaucracy on the one hand
and a mysterious allegory of universal pitfalls on the
other. It is a metaphysical comedy in which tricky
camerawork and fleet ballet maneuvers of style bear
the stamp of a technical master who has an occasional
Irish weakness for blarney. Wit sometimes descends
into whimsey. Completely original, it paradoxically
brings to mind, as so many less original works do not,

the world and the tone of other writers, and of Joyce and *Finnegans Wake* in particular. (A one-legged man who first tries to murder the narrator and then befriends him is named Finnucane.) Though O'Brien's book makes no claim to the grandeur and sweep of Joyce's epic, its hero is dead, Joyce's asleep; both books are circular in construction, slyly erudite in a similar fashion, and depend for a good deal of their force and comedy on linguistic invention. The outsize, cardboard caricatures of the three policemen suggest Kafka's "assistants" in managing simultaneously to appear both innocent and forbidding, and their cryptic dialogue owes more than a little to *Alice in Wonderland*.

O'Brien belongs to a school of fiction more interested in archetype than in character and in metamorphosis than in action. His puppetlike figures do not suffer as individuals in any ordinary sense; they suffer for everyone in some general amusement park of the soul while confronting their unexpected fates. In O'Brien's hell, guilt is a moral implication, not a matter of psychological anguish, and intimidation is the major terror, not humiliation. O'Brien mines and transforms; he takes the weather of other writers and creates a climate of his own. *The Third Policeman,* written in Ireland in 1940 and published here twenty-seven years later, is both *sui generis* and the product of a literary convention. And for no reason one can definitely point to, it is as strangely emotionally affecting as it is funny.

[1968]

Leo Tolstoy
Happy Families
Are All Alike

Two stories are told in *Anna Karenina*
—Anna's and Levin's. Yet the overall design of the
novel does not require the two major characters to
confront one another dramatically. Anna and Levin
meet only once, and they meet to no purpose relevant
to the destinies of either. We have two parallel plots.
What is the point of Levin's story in relation to Anna's?

In earlier drafts of the novel, Levin did not appear
at all; the book was exclusively Anna's. What made
Tolstoy add another strand to the rope? To give a
fuller picture of Russian life in the 1870's? Enlarging
the canvas merely for the sake of enlargement would
seem unlikely. Tolstoy had only recently completed
War and Peace. The exquisite attention Tolstoy pays
to working out the parallels of the two stories, the fine-
ness of detail everywhere, suggests some other motive

at work. At the end of the novel, we are focused on Levin and find we have been engaged in a spiritual search. The original question changes: What is the point of *Anna*'s story in relation to Levin's?

The famous first sentence of the novel—"Happy families are all alike; every unhappy family is unhappy in its own way"—does not lack for illustration. There are four major examples, each designed to illustrate the point:

The Oblonskys—where the husband, Stepan Arkayevitch, is unfaithful to his wife Dolly.

The Karenins—where the wife, Anna, is unfaithful to her husband Alexey.

The Vronskys—where Anna and Vronsky are unfaithful to the tenets of society and each sacrifices the possibility of an alternate happiness: Anna gives up her husband and child; Vronsky his possible marriage to Kitty and his career.

The Levins—where both partners are faithful.

Other characters thwart society's conventions but do not threaten its foundations: Count Vronsky's mother, who is notorious for her affairs; Princess Betsy Tverskoy and her illicit attachment to Tushkevich; and so on. Certain relationships are so far beyond the borders of what society thinks possible that they do not constitute a threat either: Nicolai, Levin's brother, and his affair with a prostitute, Masha.

Out of self-interest, society tolerates a discreet sexual liaison—its members are all in the same boat—but punishes one that openly threatens its pretended standards. Stiva is more upset because his affair with the governess is discovered than because he feels any sense of guilt. Alexey Karenin, in regard to Anna and Vronsky, is more concerned with public appearance than private anguish. Anna is not capable of concealment or discretion; she is destroyed by the forces of society, themselves decadent and corrupt.

But there is more to be said on the subject. Society's values operate within Anna—she is not an intellectual or a rebel by nature. Primarily, Anna is done in by the single-mindedness of her passion. As it slowly becomes an obsession, she lets go of every other consideration. Since she has chosen (or seems to have chosen) to exist outside the pale of society, what she chooses to exist by must make up for the pleasures and power of society itself. As her relationship with Vronsky fails, there is no one and no place to turn back to; the sheltering trees of family, society, and even God have been uprooted.

When Vronsky's horse, Frou-Frou, breaks his leg in the race and Vronsky is thrown, Anna—by her display of emotion reacting to Vronsky's danger—is forced to offer some explanation to Alexey about the cause of her agitation, and she tells him the truth about her relationship to Vronsky. The inability to hide emotion is fatal in a society that depends on appearances. What is natural and what is social are opposed. When Anna almost dies giving birth, there is a spiritual enlargement of Vronsky and Alexey in the face of death.

They become human beings, not social mannequins; threatened by loss, they give up their rivalry and join forces. Alexey forgives Vronsky. Temporarily. The trouble is, of course, that Anna does not die.

Though society may depend on appearances, it is because nature overrides society that Anna and Levin are so connected in the reader's mind, even though they meet only once. Levin, naïvely prepared to meet a "bad woman," finds Anna sympathetic in every way. The parallel plots perform a subterranean function: ideally, the two people in the novel most congenial to one another are Anna and Levin. Though they do not know it, the reader senses it. They are the only two people in a cast that comes to include hundreds who are willing to sacrifice their lives to honesty—emotional or spiritual. Neither can exist by a social code; neither is directed in major actions by forces and people from without. They are responsive, think and feel for themselves, have equally delicate sensibilities and minds, and are both in forced states of rebellion. Anna revolts against a sexual code not as a bluestocking but out of necessity; Levin, being aware of larger values, flouts the social conventions because he cannot accept them. Both are obviously "good" characters. We believe in the purity of their motives at every point in the novel.

In some ways, Levin comes off better as a character. He is "scenic" before he is dramatic; he is glimpsed, caught at the odd moment (his remark about turbot), perceived in small actions, developed gradually and leisurely, whereas Anna appears in the midst of a crisis that almost immediately becomes her own. Before Levin gets involved in any crucial action, we know a great deal about him. And though we never question Anna's charm, beauty, or intelligence, these qualities are not to be the source of her agony—which is the result of a special capacity for love. She is plunged headlong into her affair with Vronsky before we can fully understand why that passion engulfs her to a degree that will ultimately prove fatal. This is partly the result of a certain "lightness" in Vronsky himself. But it is primarily the result of a foreshortening of perspective at the beginning of the novel, where one must take on faith who Anna is. Why is she so susceptible to Vronsky, and why is her relationship to him the all-or-nothing involvement it becomes? We know the answer by the time the novel ends; what I am suggesting is that we do not know it in time, and this leads to certain difficulties later. There is, for instance, a certain lack of credibility in Anna's willingness to give up Seryozha, the son she adores. And the precipitousness of her affair lacks credibility, too, at the time it occurs in relation to the total time-scheme of the novel. Why did not Anna allow herself a lighthearted version of this kind of release before, considering the stultifying pompousness of her husband? The answer might be: that is not the kind of woman Anna is. And the rebuttal to the answer might be: Why do we not know what kind of woman Anna is?

On the other hand, we see Levin disappointed and badly hurt by Kitty's rejection, and we know something of his impulsiveness, his integrity, and his shyness by the time he is involved in a spiritual crisis. And that crisis can be isolated without further exposition. We know Levin before he is in the drama; we get to know Anna through her involvement in the drama. The canon of the novel would suggest the latter to be a superior method. But that is not so in this case. For *Anna Karenina* is not a Jamesian novel of moral subtlety in which the threads of the drama are pulled tight and a mystery finally unraveled, where sensibility and tension tremble upon a question mark. It is a novel built event upon event and scene by scene, in which the very lack of conflict between the two major characters prevents a certain kind of drama from operating. Levin remains in proportion to the episodic and cumulative effect of Tolstoy's style. Anna does not. Anna's drama within Levin's epic is diminished by it and the very breadth of portraiture that extends to character and action in the novel is absent from Tolstoy's treatment of Anna *up to the point* of her sleeping with Vronsky. That major dramatic action lacks force at the time it occurs. Levin comes to us slowly, Anna quickly, and we understand him better because of it. If one could conceive of the novel being placed on the stage, there would be something slightly false or difficult to explain in Anna's succumbing to Vronsky so quickly. Levin's story would present no such dramatic difficulty.

But Levin's story would present us with a difficulty of another kind. If Anna is foreshortened at the beginning, the complexity of Levin's thought is rather flatly resolved at the end. There are two weaknesses in *Anna Karenina*: one dramatic—a character is brought to crisis too quickly; and one thematic—a crisis is too easily resolved.

But these two weaknesses are the defects of an amazing success. It is impossible to think of another writer who, in doggedly piling up chronological events, in running in and out of his characters' minds with the same felicity with which he describes a horse race, a tree, a dress, and so on, could so definitively avoid the problem of viewpoint by ignoring it. There is the confidence of genius overriding all difficulties in *Anna Karenina* and the reader knows it—knows he is in the hands of a master. There is nothing the author is incapable of putting down. One of the strange effects of this genius is to make "psychology" and "nature" inseparable. The transition between a description of a leaf and somebody's thoughts is unnoticeable. The physical energy, the power of the style suggests, finally, that all phenomena are made of the same texture. Some kind of mental unity binds all things together. We are overwhelmed by the truth everywhere of what Tolstoy sees and says. In that sense, *Anna Karenina* resists criticism to the same degree that life resists theory. If what Henry James called "felt experience" did not saturate the pages of *Anna Karenina* with an absolute fidelity to life, the beginning with its cramped exposition, and the ending, with its dubious moral resolution, would mar the total picture.

Small parallels of action are important in the over-all design:

The deaths, for instance. The guard who is killed at the train station when Anna and Vronsky meet for the first time obviously prefigures the death of Anna herself.

As Kitty falls, Anna rises. As Anna falls, Kitty rises.

As Anna comes to help reconcile Dolly and Stiva, so Stiva comes to help reconcile Anna and Alexey.

It is Mme. Vronsky who is proud that Vronsky associates himself with a woman of Anna's class and type. And it is she who comes to loathe Anna and to see her as a degrading and destructive influence on her son. It is Kitty's mother, the Princess, who dislikes Levin for Kitty and then comes to want Kitty to marry Levin.

These ambiguities, which are a process of life and take time to reveal themselves, are fixed in a quicker breeding ground in the character and temperament of Nicolai, Levin's brother, where the changes of mood and feeling occur minute by minute.

Anna Karenina is full of examples of spiritual humbug, and various religious revelations and conversions take place that turn out to be false. Alexey in the scene where Anna almost dies; Kitty and Mme. Stahl. Alexey's spiritual dilemma is the opposite of Kitty's. Alexey, who lives by the world alone, comes to a spiritual condition of goodness only to have the world wrest it from him by its demands. Kitty, trying to give the world up, finds it mirrored in Mme. Stahl.

The importance of Tolstoy's fairness to Alexander Karenin. We dislike him; we are never able to hate him.

The good nurses never change: Dolly's nurse, who fixes the summer house; Levin's nurse, who cares for him at his estate.

It would be almost impossible to separate the Anna from the Levin story. If we could, we would have something like an untidy *Madame Bovary*.

Tolstoy sees humiliation as the most disintegrating factor of identity throughout. For Proust, that factor is obsession. Tolstoy is not concerned with art. Oddly, there are no artists in *Anna Karenina*.

Anna Karenina begins with a common garden variety of adultery and goes on to an adultery that transforms several lives and leads to a tragic death. The minor announcement of the major subject lures us on with a secret hope. We keep wishing that Anna would or could get out of her situation as easily as Stiva got out of his.

The peculiar fact of Anna and Vronsky having the same dream: the peasant who bends down and speaks French.

The extraordinary nature scenes—snipe shooting, the mowing (the scene about the water cup), Laska, the horses, the race—all provide an undercurrent to the action. They remind us of the biological underpinnings of life, which no amount of civilization can destroy. Our last glimpse of Vronsky as a soldier going off to the war makes another point: civilization can destroy itself. Though Anna and society are at odds, they are both at the mercy of a similar force: self-destruction.

[1968]

Elizabeth Bowen
Intelligence at War

The pleasures of an Elizabeth Bowen novel are evident in her new one, *Eva Trout, or Changing Scenes*: the wit, the virtuosity of style (the envy of writers who cannot emulate it, the delight of readers who do not have to), the hard-grained intelligence, the understanding of the most subtle feelings. Miss Bowen can pin down the elusive in a phrase. What she doesn't know about the way things look or the insides of people seems hardly worth knowing. Very few writers as intelligent as she are equally sympathetic. The mind is cool, not cold. The heart is warm, not sticky.

Yet, for all her virtues, Miss Bowen is an unfashionable writer at the moment. There are reasons. She has been pigeonholed as a writer of "sensibility"—a depictor of emotional states, with a special insight into the horrors of love. This misconception has its roots in *The Death of the Heart,* her most famous novel. Justly admired for the perfection of its form and style, it has been widely misread. It is not a sentimental novel but an ironic one, whose action turns and comments upon itself deliberately. In one crucial scene, its main character, Portia Quayne, upon whom so much compassion has been expended, is revealed from new angles: as a bore and as a threat. Moreover, *The Death of the Heart* is not merely a novel of "adolescence." Two contending forces wrestle in it for the possession of a soul: one is primitive and beneficial (Matchett, the Quaynes's housekeeper); the other is clever and malevolent (St. Quentin Miller, a writer).

And then, Miss Bowen is not after the representative person, but the representative experience. There are all kinds of hell. Her collection of stories, *Ivy Gripped the Steps,* and her novel, *The Heat of the Day,* provide the best portrait I know of wartime London. Yet in both, the general must be assumed through the particular. With one possible exception, none of the characters in *The Heat of the Day* is the representative of a group. Its author's diagnosis of middle-class values that lead to the making of a traitor is important (at the time the novel was published, no one saw how important it was going to *become*), but those values are not *only* middle-class. In short, for Miss Bowen, evil can be sociological, but never merely sociological. In the same novel, the subtle links established between a character judged to be insane and the supposedly healthy middle-class Kelway family exemplify the kind of intelligence that permeates her fiction—an intelligence of intrinsic values not easily reducible to abstract generalization.

Miss Bowen handles ideas through the scrim of conventional façades. She *writes* as if civilization still existed, but by dealing so insistently with dislocation and corruption, her novels question the assumption. In her work, the tone of what is being said, and what is being said, are not always the same.

The central figure in *Eva Trout* is a large, awkward girl, the heiress to a fortune so big no one really knows its dimensions. She is unformed and an outsider by nature. Her past is murky; her present indecisive; she has no grip on the future. Her mother died in a plane crash; her father committed suicide. Her father's lover, Constantine, has been her guardian ever since she was a child. We meet her, a few months before she is to come into her inheritance, at the shore of a lake surrounding a castle. The castle belongs to Constantine, who has conveniently arranged for Eva to stay with the Arbles, a married couple down on their luck, the owners of a plum orchard in Worchestshire. Iseult Arble, Eva's former teacher, took Eva on as an experiment in humanization—an experiment, it turns out, that cut both ways. The shaping influence of Eva's life, Iseult, like most idols, is worshiped, then repudiated.

Though Eva is the Arbles's transient guest, she spends most of her time at the vicarage, the home of the Dancey family. One of the Dancey sons, Henry—precocious, seemingly helpless but with a genuine force—is to become Eva's pretended, then real fiancé later in the novel. Before he does, we are taken on an international pilgrimage: Eva's search for her self and a place to house it in. She eventually goes to America, adopts a child, Jeremy, and discovers he is a deaf-mute. She brings him back to London, back to the old com-

plicities of Iseult and Constantine, a metaphysical vaude-
ville team who once guided her destinies and now have
come to have their destinies guided by her. Jeremy is
kidnapped by a disguised Iseult; a sculptress, a priest,
and a doctor are woven briefly into the action; the
complications multiply; and the novel races on to a
hair-raising, melodramatic conclusion.

Eva's conversational style is described as "cement-
like"; if life has any secrets, she does not seem to know
them. She is by turns taciturn, enigmatic—and of a
surprising wisdom. She possesses the special but unpre-
dictable awareness of certain kinds of inarticulate people; sometimes she seems to know much less than anyone around her, sometimes infinitely more. Through
a nearsighted inability to foresee consequences, with
the best of intentions, or none, she creates chaos around
her. She is constantly being interpreted; the accuracy
of the translations is always in question.

The first thing she says is a lie—she mentions a hon-
eymoon that has never taken place—but she is not a
liar as much as a role player unable to distinguish between romance and fact. To Eva, a sort of radar station searching the horizon for clues to her existence,
anything and everything seems possible. In a perpetual
state of metamorphosis, she infects others: the view she
takes of the world is the view they take of her. Since
she has no shape, everyone wants to shape her. She is
the kindest of monsters. Her identity being uncertain,
she manages to make all identity uncertain.

Eva's relationship to Jeremy exists in counterpoint
to Iseult's relationship to Eva. Unloved, but capable of
loving, Eva is a child who plays at being a mother.

The results are devastating. Having been controlled, she becomes an unwitting controller. In most Bowen novels, and in this one, the seemingly powerless exert power. The damage inflicted on the innocent and the damage inflicted by them are equal; lethal blows are exchanged on both sides. In *Eva Trout,* there is a continuing series of manipulations by the childless of a child.

Wider meanings are suggested. The one definitive action in the book is made by a character who never speaks. Words lie, but the lack of them is equally atrocious. Vocabularies are our fated traps; they not only express our misapprehensions, they compound them. But without them, we move into the idylls of pure mindlessness or pure violence. Because words or the lack of them is its very subject, the style of the novel owes everything to its theme: intelligence is at war with the inarticulated cry. The verbal brilliance of its outer circles reveals, at its center, a speechless child.

Different from earlier Bowen novels, which owed something to the drama in their construction, *Eva Trout* moves with the flickering rapidity of the movie camera. We are transported quickly from place to place, from character to character. A certain hallucinatory aura, more common to Miss Bowen's short stories than to her novels, rises from its pages. And the variations in speed dampen the shock effect of the ending. A virtuoso balancing act between the comic and the intense, the novel is uneven. In one chapter, Iseult sits down at her desk and types out everything she thinks. The chapter is brilliant. Another chapter, a jab at midwestern vulgarity, seems to me completely mistaken.

An air of the quixotic hangs over the work as a whole, as if a master architect had tilted the angle of a building a bit or added a stained-glass window or two not quite in keeping with the original plan.

Miss Bowen's new novel makes it clear once again that she is in an odd position as a writer. Over a long period of time, her work has been produced against the background of her individual conscience—unrecognized because it is not the same at all as a sense of guilt—a conscience that has not been devoured by the self. She writes as she pleases and suffers the consequences. None of her novels has been made into a movie; she has won no international literary prizes. Ignored by Los Angeles and Stockholm equally, she is one of the few writers who could make equal claims on both. Like Henry James, she is a storyteller in the most primitive sense and a writer in the most profound one.

[1968]

A Note About the Author

Howard Moss is the author of one previous volume of criticism, *The Magic Lantern of Marcel Proust,* and six books of poems, the most recent of which is *Second Nature,* published in the fall of 1968. He has written several plays, including *The Palace at 4 A.M., The Oedipus Mah-Jongg Scandal,* and *The Folding Green.*

Mr. Moss was born in 1922 in New York City, where he still lives. After teaching at Vassar, he joined the staff of *The New Yorker* in 1948 and has been its poetry editor since 1950. He has received several fellowships for his writing, including two to the MacDowell Colony, and in 1968 he received a literature grant from the National Institute of Arts and Letters.